The New Silversmith

The New Silversmith

Innovative, Sustainable Techniques for
Creating Nature-Inspired Jewelry

Nicole Ringgold

QUARRY

Quarto.com

© 2024 Quarto Publishing Group USA Inc.
Text © 2024 Nicole A. Ringgold
Photography © Cymone L. Van Marter

First Published in 2024 by Quarry Books, an imprint of The Quarto Group,
100 Cummings Center, Suite 265-D, Beverly, MA 01915, USA.
T (978) 282-9590 F (978) 283-2742

Quarry Books titles are also available at discount for retail, wholesale, promotional, and bulk purchase. For details, contact the Special Sales Manager by email at specialsales@quarto.com or by mail at The Quarto Group, Attn: Special Sales Manager, 100 Cummings Center, Suite 265-D, Beverly, MA 01915, USA.

10 9 8 7 6 5 4 3 2 1

ISBN: 978-0-7603-8569-2

Digital edition published in 2024
eISBN: 978-0-7603-8570-8

Library of Congress Cataloging-in-Publication Data
Names: Ringgold, Nicole, author.
Title: The new silversmith : innovative, sustainable techniques for
  creating nature-inspired jewelry / Nicole Ringgold.
Description: Beverly : Quarry, 2024. | Includes index.
Identifiers: LCCN 2023056331 (print) | LCCN 2023056332 (ebook) | ISBN
  9780760385692 (hardcover) | ISBN 9780760385708 (ebook)
Subjects: LCSH: Jewelry making. | Silver jewelry.
Classification: LCC TT212 .R564 2024 (print) | LCC TT212 (ebook) | DDC
  739.27--dc23/eng/20240102
LC record available at https://lccn.loc.gov/2023056331
LC ebook record available at https://lccn.loc.gov/2023056332

Design: Amy Sly, The Sly Studio
Page Layout: Emily Austin, The Sly Studio

Printed in China

Dedication

For Martha (Foreman) Haldimann, my seventh-grade
special education teacher, who was the first person
to tell me that art is a form of intelligence. I cannot
imagine where I would be without the confidence she
helped instill in me. I will be forever grateful.

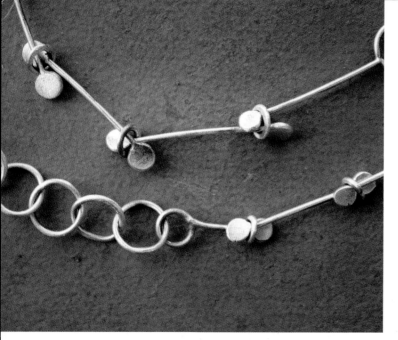

Contents

"Spoon feeding in the long run teaches us nothing but the shape of the spoon."
—E. M. FOSTER, *THE OBSERVER*, OCTOBER 7, 1951

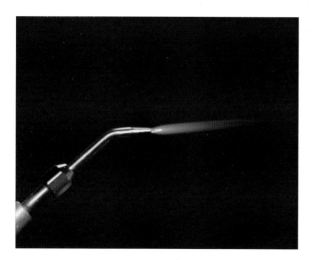

Preface

ALMOST EVERYTHING I KNOW ABOUT SILVERSMITHING I GAINED THROUGH TRIAL AND ERROR.
Brainstorming and successfully executing a design brings me enormous satisfaction. I've also unearthed my love for teaching in untraditional ways, using tactile exercises, visual diagrams, guiltless repetition, adaptive terminology, and any other modality that works best for each individual. In return, I'm honored to witness the pride and elation I see with every one of my students' accomplishments.

The New Silversmith is a story of discovery. It's an extension of my profound passion to teach and help others acquire knowledge in new, provocative ways. It's an account of how I uncovered, in unconventional means and through countless mishaps, a world that brings me immense joy. Together, let's learn.

Overview

To understand this book, it's important to first understand my process. Much of how I work with precious metal is outside anything you'll learn from another metalsmithing book or workshop. My motto is this: "I try it myself before I believe in impossibilities."

You may have been told that it's impossible to fuse sterling silver. That simply isn't true. Many of my sculptural pieces are built on a fused and carved sterling silver foundation, such as a dragonfly thorax, clamshell, or tree bark. Throughout this book, I'll dissect and help you navigate each step, giving you insight into an entirely different way of working with metal.

Another distinctive practice I've implemented in my work is how to diagnose torch control by reading the colors of sterling silver. By the time you have completed each of the exercises in this book, you too will be able to discern why your solder didn't flow, where you focused the heat of your torch, and whether or not your piece still contains flux, all by watching the colors of the silver change.

Finally, for those of you who are as concerned as I am about incorporating chemicals into your everyday work, you'll learn how to minimize your exposure by utilizing heat sinks. Rather than seeing them as an impediment, you'll understand how to use them to your benefit to prevent previous solder joints from reflowing.

Although this book is geared toward metalsmiths with intermediate to advanced experience, there is something here for everyone, including how to fuse basic chains, fabricate branches, forge a leaf, and so much more. I hope that you, too, will try it yourself before you believe in impossibilities.

A Note about the QR codes

Throughout the book you'll find QR codes that allow you to access short excerpts from my series of video tutorials (see the Resources for more information). Each video excerpt focuses on the content shown on the page or spread on which the QR code appears.

My Journey

I WAS A STUDENT WHO STRUGGLED TO LEARN and thrive within the boundaries of mainstream education. I didn't adequately learn to read until fifth grade when my mother thankfully forced me to sit in the kitchen every night to read out loud while she prepared dinner. When I did read proficiently, I despised studying anything that required memorizing a textbook. I highlighted hundreds of words and concepts but retained very few. My notebooks were filled with elaborate doodles, and my teachers continuously remarked that my head was forever "in the clouds."

In middle school, I was pulled from class every week to work with a special education teacher who administered standardized achievement tests. She encouraged me to write creatively, play a musical instrument, and draw. She recognized and helped me understand that I was a gifted artist and that being an artist was a form of intelligence. She ultimately changed my life, but at that time, I was still floundering in the system.

My lifelong dream was to be an artist. However, to make a living as one I was told that I would have to teach art or have a second, more prominent job to generate income until my portfolio was discovered. Even *if* I was discovered, there was no guarantee a salary would be consistent or sustainable, so it was a risky profession. As a result, I earned my undergraduate degree in Sociology and Studio Art, anticipating a lifetime of balancing both. Hence, I pushed on through school.

I spent three years in the Peace Corps in Niger, West Africa, where I was encouraged to teach using body language, visual aids, and through hands-on workshops. I organized a youth group to teach village children how to compost and garden. During a March 8th Women's Day celebration, I recruited women from surrounding villages to share their knowledge of soap and bread making. I spent countless hours with my best friend—a deaf twelve-year-old boy—giving him Geography and World History lessons with postcards, through our self-concocted sign language, and his remarkable ability to read lips. The most profound aspect of my Peace Corps experience was not what I was able to teach, but how much I learned.

I returned to the United States to earn my graduate degree in Art Therapy and Mental Health Counseling where I finally understood that I abhor regimented learning, but I absolutely love to learn.

I worked for almost fifteen years managing social service programs and directing nonprofit organizations, all the while dabbling in a variety of art forms and doing what I could to feed my thirst for a creative outlet.

When we built our home in 2009, my husband and I incorporated my art throughout: glass and stone mosaics, an elaborate mural in our daughter's bedroom, and another one on our pantry door. I drilled holes through river rocks I had collected to create cabinet knobs. When the house was complete, I continued to drill (much smaller) rocks and taught myself how to wire wrap jewelry. My daily life balance included being a wife, mother, nonprofit director, homeowner, gardener, outdoor enthusiast, and suddenly a determined jewelry artist.

In 2011, I opened an Etsy store, my first step in online sales. For the next three years, I sold jewelry through Etsy and local galleries. I slowly expanded gallery support from my small town in north central Washington to western Washington and surrounding states. With the income from my jewelry sales, I purchased my first torch and eventually managed to furnish my studio with basic silversmithing tools and equipment. Every day after work, dinner, and debriefing with my family, I would retreat to my studio to work late into the evening, teaching myself new techniques with the torch and tools I had acquired. Without any formal instruction, I learned through making mistakes and giving myself personal challenges, such as 100 hand fabricated chains. By 2014, I was optimistic that over the next three years I could continue working full-time as the director of a nonprofit organization and save one year's worth of salary from my jewelry sales so that I could quit my job in 2017 and have a year's worth of income to fall back on should my artist venture take time to generate any sort of substantial income.

However, tragedy changed my plans. In 2014, a wildfire swept through our neighborhood, burning our home and my studio. All was gone. Overwhelmed by our loss and overcome with grief, we faced the reality that we owned only what we were wearing that day. With disaster came the realization that we could either reinvent our wheel or we could take the opportunity to shrink our lifestyle and leap forward to grasp any opportunity that we'd previously bypassed because our lives were already too full. It was then that my husband encouraged me to quit my day job and finally pursue my dream of becoming an artist.

Fortunately, a local greenhouse opened its doors to me, an ideal space for my new silversmithing studio. With abundant natural light and year-round plants growing in all corners, I never experienced a lack of inspiration. Every day that I entered my studio I found new inspiration: a dragonfly, butterfly, croaking frog, ladybugs, and a plethora of plants.

After the fire, my husband and I purchased a small home, and thankfully, I received a grant from CERF+ (originally called Craft Emergency Relief Fund, now known as The Artist's Safety Net) to help with the reinvestment in tools and equipment. I quit my job and dove headfirst into silversmithing. To say it was a challenging first year is an understatement.

While juggling the logistics of home insurance, renewing passports, birth certificates, repurchasing clothes, home furnishings, and getting ourselves back on our feet, I was struggling to find my voice as an artist. I couldn't figure out how to set myself apart from the millions of other jewelry artists selling online, sharing their work on Etsy, Pinterest, and other social media platforms. We all seemed to be making similar pieces and pursuing the same market. Even though my work was selling, I went into debt. I entertained the idea of building a wholesale business, but was daunted by the world of wholesale shows and bulk orders. I began to spiral. In the fall of 2015, I shut down my Etsy shop and Pinterest account and took several days to hike, breathe, and collect my thoughts.

While I was trail running, it dawned on me: I was going to create botanicals in silver. I had seen countless cast plants incorporated into jewelry designs, but never had I seen hand-fabricated plant jewelry. To build the skill set required, I challenged myself to make thirty botanicals. I spent the next three months dissecting thirty different plants and re-creating them in silver. By doing so, I improved my soldering skills, learned how to form and manipulate metal, and discovered so many out-of-the-box techniques. I opened a website, joined Instagram, and my work finally caught the attention it needed to establish myself as a notable artist.

I have now been a full-time silversmith for eight years. I continue to push and challenge myself, and I thoroughly enjoy teaching and sharing the skills I've mastered. I hope to continue traveling widely to teach and inspire aspiring silversmiths, sharing these three messages: First, there is no one way to teach or to learn. Second, try things for yourself before you believe in impossibilities. And third, it *is*, in fact, possible to make a comfortable living as an artist.

The
Essentials

Rules: Let's Talk About Safety

IT CAN BE HUMILIATING TO ENTER SOMEONE'S STUDIO without any prior understanding of their rules, only to be scolded as if you should have known better. It was witnessing one of these encounters that clued me into the fact that many metalsmiths worry that their files will be compromised if used in two directions. This surprised me because my presumption was that files were double cut and could be used in a back-and-forth motion. I didn't dispute the issue because they weren't my files, and it wasn't my studio. Instead, I made a mental note to familiarize myself with basic rules applied across the board so as not to verbally (or physically) stumble, get hurt, or worse, be held liable.

Admittedly, I tend to be lax with rules in my own studio. Throughout the summer, I prefer to be barefoot or, at the very least, wear open-toed shoes. I keep a lit candle on my bench to ignite my torch. I place wet metal on my anvil. And yes, I do use my files in both directions. Yet, many of the rules you'll encounter exist for a reason, and it's pertinent for each one to become habitual.

I asked for input from our metalsmithing community to help me compile a comprehensive list of rules. I've broken that list down into two parts: Safety Rules and Other Rules.

Safety Rules

You must wear close-toed shoes.

If you have long hair, tie it up.

Do not wear loose-fitted clothing or dangling jewelry.

Wear an apron to protect your clothing and skin.

Wear safety glasses.

Wear appropriate personal protective equipment, such as a respirator and a rubber/plastic apron when handling acids and chemicals, and chemical-resistant gloves.

Do not use a cigarette lighter to ignite your torch.

Have a current fire extinguisher at the ready in your studio.

Shut down tanks and bleed hoses at the end of each shift.

Do not leave a flame on between projects (which includes the pilot light).

Ensure that there is adequate studio ventilation.

Other Rules

You must file only in one direction or else you'll compromise your files.

Do not place wet metal or tools on an anvil.

Using magnetic holders to store your hand tools will ruin their magnetism.

Tumbling will work-harden your finished pieces.

You must hold your torch with your nondominant hand.

The list is overwhelming. But are all the rules legitimate or necessary? The short answer is both yes and no. Yes, they are all legitimate. No, they are not all necessary. Even if you choose not to implement the entire list of rules in your own studio, it's important to recognize and not judge that other metalsmiths may be more safety conscious than you are, may be more concerned about their tools, and may strictly adhere to every single bullet point on the above lists.

The Metal

WHILE GIVING WORKSHOPS, I'm often asked why I use sterling silver rather than fine silver or Argentium.

To clarify, the fineness of a precious metal object (coin, bar, jewelry, etc.) translates to the weight by ounce of fine metal in proportion to the total weight, which may also include alloying base metals and other impurities. Alloy metals are added to increase the hardness and durability of coins and jewelry, alter colors, or decrease cost. For example, copper is added to fine silver to make a more durable alloy for use in coins, housewares, and jewelry.

Sterling silver is an alloy of silver containing 92.5% by weight of silver and 7.5% by weight of other metals, usually copper. The sterling silver standard has a minimum millesimal fineness (purity) of 925 (which means in parts per 1,000, 925 must be pure silver).

Fine silver has a millesimal fineness of 999. Also called pure silver, fine silver contains 99.9% silver, with the balance being trace amounts of impurities. Today, fine silver is generally considered to be too soft for general use. Due to its softness, it's an excellent option for chasing and repoussé, as well as fusing and enameling.

Argentium, originally patented in 1998, is a tarnish-resistant silver that contains 93.5% or 96% silver. Metalloid germanium in Argentium replaces the copper alloys in the traditional sterling silver. The benefits of using Argentium include (but are not limited to) fire scale elimination, tarnish resistance, precipitation and simple heat-hardening properties, and fusing.

Given this information, why do I use sterling silver? My short answer is simple: I prefer the finished color of sterling silver.

Yet, there's quite a bit more to my story.

If you're reading this as a metalsmith, perhaps you can relate to the feeling of overwhelm when picking up your first wholesale mail-order catalogue or scrolling through a wholesaler's website, completely bewildered about what gauge sheet or wire to purchase. It made zero sense to me why the numbers increased while the gauge of metal decreased. I didn't understand hard versus soft, sterling versus fine, nor the fluctuating weight by ounce.

My initial precious metal purchases were experimental, some of which remained permanently untouched. When I set my first stone, I used hand sheers purchased at our local hardware store to cut through 22-gauge sterling silver sheet. It didn't dawn on me until after that first stone setting endeavor that I should use a softer, lighter-gauge silver. It was then that I learned about fine silver and bezel wire. Even still, I didn't know what dimensions to buy, and I rolled and burnished my settings with a knitting needle until I discovered the roller and burnisher.

All of this occurred before even considering what drill bits and burs I should use. But I delve into those details later in this chapter (see page 25).

Over time, I developed a preference for gauge and malleability based on each project, and I grew enchanted with sterling silver. I love how it can be rigid and fixed into precise geometric shapes, or it can be softened and manipulated into organic forms. Discovering the benefits of annealing was a game changer. I stumbled upon fusing sterling silver, which is now a core component of my work. It took countless hours of trial and error until I reached a point where I understood exactly how much to heat a mass while soldering multiple tiny components and utilizing heat sinks. I learned to interpret the metal's chemistry based on feel and color.

Let's take a look at the colors of sterling silver.

The Colors of Sterling Silver

The following are the *Color Codes* as I see them while working with sterling silver.

Steps Before Soldering

First, it's important to note how I prepare my metal before soldering (my system changes when fusing). I do not wash or scrub the silver beforehand. I anneal, pickle, quench, and dry it.

Second, keep in mind what prevents solder from flowing:

1. Dirt, such as dust, fingerprints, or excess flux.

2. Too little heat.

3. No flux, which can occur by not applying flux in the first place or by a higher ratio of oxygen to gas, which will burn off the flux before the solder has a chance to flow.

Gray

When gray, sterling silver can be one or all of the following: dirty, hard, or brittle.

Even if you purchase dead-soft silver sheet, there is a chance it's covered with dust or fingerprints. Annealing will ensure that it's both clean and soft.

Pickling after annealing isn't essential, but I do so religiously, as I've found that it allows me to better observe the change in its color as it's worked.

Once you have annealed and pickled your silver, you may choose to form it. As you do, it'll become increasingly gray as it becomes brittle. You'll also notice that your silver is unresponsive to your attempts at forming. You'll need to re-anneal to soften before continuing to form. If you continue to form without annealing, your silver will likely crack or tear.

White

White indicates that the silver has been annealed and pickled. It is clean and malleable.

Yellow

I'm a big fan of My-T-Flux (liquid hard-soldering flux) because it can be lightly applied and helps prevent fire scale. I also prefer to flux everything my torch touches (not just the spot where I want the solder to flow) so that I can continue to watch the colors transform as I'm heating the mass (more on that later).

Gray sterling silver.

White sterling silver.

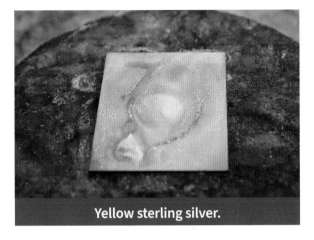

Yellow sterling silver.

Black sterling silver.

Once your silver has been annealed, pickled, and fluxed, as you heat your piece, the flux will "foam" and then turn a subtle yellow hue. This is the "solder flow point." The speed at which your solder will flow depends on what hardness of solder you're using, yet you'll find that, once your silver turns yellow, your solder will soon flow.

Black

Black silver means that it has oxidized.

Note. If your sterling silver has been depletion-gilded (annealed approximately 10 times), you should be watching for a soft rose color instead of black.

If you forget to flux your piece before heating, your silver will skip the yellow stage and immediately turn from white to black. If this happens, at the very least, STOP. Turn off your torch. Let your silver cool. Apply flux and continue. However, I prefer to STOP, turn off my torch, *pickle my piece*, and then apply flux and continue. Pickling allows me to monitor the changing color.

If you applied flux before heating and the silver transforms from white to yellow to black, you have done everything right, but you have burned off your flux. If this occurs before the solder has had a chance to flow, it's usually a sign that you are using too much oxygen. If this happens, STOP. Turn off your torch. Re-anneal and pickle your piece. Apply flux. Ensure that you have the appropriate ratio of oxygen and fuel and continue.

Red sterling silver.

Red

Red is the silver's melting point. If your intention is to solder, not to reticulate or melt a hole in your silver sheet, STOP. Turn off your torch. Re-anneal and pickle your piece. Apply flux. Ensure that you have the appropriate flame and continue.

If your intention is to reticulate, melt a hole in your silver sheet, or fuse your sterling silver, this is where that magic begins. We'll delve into this later in the book (see page 133).

I encourage you to repeatedly experiment with sterling silver until you can recognize the changes in color. To start, grab some sterling silver scrap and try the exercises on the following pages.

Annealing Exercises

Exercise 1: How Does Annealing Impact Your Silver?

1. Before annealing your silver sheet, lightly paint or spray My-T-Flux across the surface. Does the flux puddle, or is it absorbed evenly across the entire surface of the metal? Using your torch, heat the metal. Realize that where the flux foams is where your solder will flow.

2. Anneal and pickle your silver. Repeat the steps above. Lightly paint or spray My-T-Flux across the surface. Does the flux puddle, or is it absorbed evenly across the entire surface of the metal? Using your torch, heat the metal. Where the flux foams is where your solder will flow. Note the difference in your metal between A and B.

For a visual example of how annealing affects silver, see the photo of "Red sterling silver" on p. 17.

Exercise 2: How Do I Identify the Solder Flow Point?

Anneal and pickle your silver scrap. Apply a light coat of flux across the entire surface. Place one small piece of each of the following on your sheet: hard, medium, easy, and extra easy solder. Using your torch, heat the metal evenly. Watch the flux foam and gel. Now, watch the color of your silver as each piece of solder balls and puddles. What colors do you see?

Exercise 3: How Long Will It Take To Melt a Hole in Silver Sheet?

I'm not sure there's anything more satisfying than deliberately melting silver. We'll explore this in future chapters. But for now, use a silver scrap that is approximately 1 inch (2.5 cm) square. No flux is needed. Point your torch directly at the center of the square. Watch the silver turn black, then red. It'll soon begin to "shiver," molten, and "pop" as a hole bursts open.

The Temperature of the Metal and the Movement of the Torch

- When you have turned on your torch, try not to wiggle the flame back and forth across your piece. Yes, you do need to consistently heat the silver, but slow down so that you have time to watch the colors of the silver change as you're heating.

- As you're heating your piece, be sure not to draw back quickly just because you're afraid that your silver will melt. If you're worried about the melting point of your silver, adjust the temperature of your flame. Slow down, breathe, and watch the silver change colors.

The Tools

WE ALL HAVE A DIFFERENT APPROACH TO EQUIPPING OUR STUDIOS. I have enviously visited a few studios that caused my jaw to hit the floor. They're decked out with every tool you could possibly dream of, with each tool spectacularly displayed on meticulous surfaces, efficient ventilation so silent you can hear a pin drop, and ample natural lighting. I've also taught in studios jam-packed with quality, heavy-duty antique tools, half of which I couldn't tell you how to use. Some silversmiths prefer to purchase as many tools as possible up front. Others, like me, make do with as little as possible until we're certain our investment will be well utilized. Of course, there is no one right way to go about it.

The bottom line is that we can be metalsmiths in very small spaces and with surprisingly few tools.

For the first two years, I worked with the same tools, partly because I tend to be a minimalist, yet also because I didn't know which tools to buy for what purpose and our finances prevented me from diving in headfirst.

My first studio was 35 square feet (3 m²). I lined the walls with wooden crates and workbenches constructed with recycled doors. I cracked open a sliding glass door for ventilation, although at that time I used honey for flux, a combination of vinegar and salt for pickle, and hardboiled eggs instead of liver of sulfur. I used knitting needles and pencils for mandrels and to burnish stone settings, and I used a combination of nails, screwdrivers, and awls for texturing.

It wasn't until after I became more serious about silversmithing that I made additional purchases.

While writing this book, I asked for input from our metalsmithing community to compile a list of unconventional tools used before investing in professionally made one. The most compelling answers were the following:

Paint sticks wrapped in sandpaper

Toothbrush for burnishing

A solid iron base for an anvil

Tow hitch and wooden door knobs for forming

Table leg for bracelet mandrel

Broom handle for doming

Recycled plastic container for tumbling

Pasta maker to flatten wire

Of course, there does come a time when we need to purchase professionally made tools. To follow along in this book, you'll need the tools shown on the following pages.

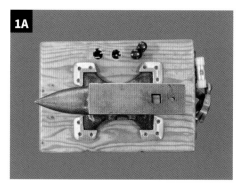

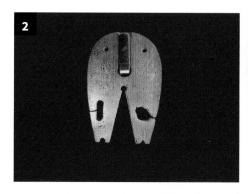

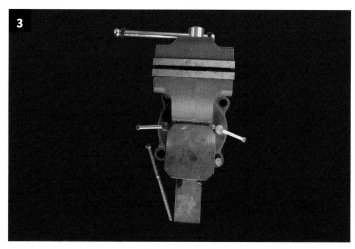

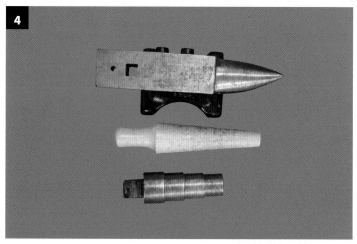

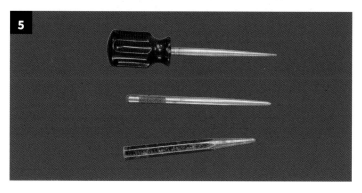

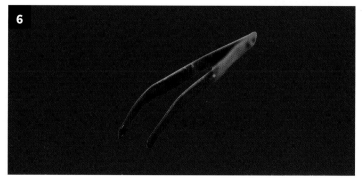

1. Anvil or steel bench block.

A. *Anvil.* A cast-iron surface used to form metal.

B. *Steel bench block.* Case-hardened steel blocks used to support your work for a variety of tasks including flattening wire, bending, riveting, and general hammering.

2. Bench pin. Optimizes access to and support of a wide variety of your workpieces, particularly when piercing and sawing.

3. Bench vise. A mechanical apparatus used to secure an object while being worked; vises have two parallel jaws, one fixed and the other movable, threaded in and out by a screw and lever.

4. Bracelet mandrel. Usually made of wood or a hardened tool steel with a smooth finish and even taper; designed for making cuffs, bangles, and other curved elements.

5. Center punch or awl. Small pointed tools used to pierce holes in or texture metal.

6. Copper tongs. Heavy-duty copper tongs are designed for safe use with pickling and acid solutions; the copper will not contaminate the pickling solution.

7. Cross-locking tweezers (insulated). Also known as shank tweezers, cross-lock titanium tweezers with heat-resistant fiber grips protect your hands from heat while working with your torch; the cross-lock mechanism opens when pressed, then closes snugly when released to grip objects securely.

8. Dapping set with block. Used to form metals into a dome shape.

9. Dedeco Sunburst Radial Discs.

10. Disc cutter. Designed to cut non-ferrous metals, disc cutters make cutting metal sheet into perfect circles simple.

11. Eastern Repoussé and Chasing Tools Set. Used to create outlines and to hammer a sheet of metal to shape metal into dimensional shapes.

12. Files. Hand files feature a larger cutting surface that is longer and wider than other file types and are ideal for fast, efficient removal of material from the workpiece for initial shaping, for smoothing and, in finer cuts, for finishing.

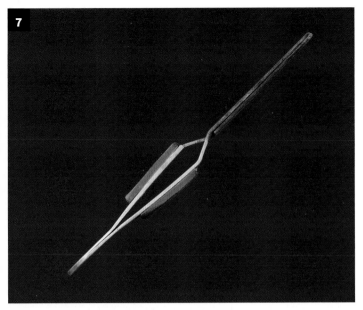

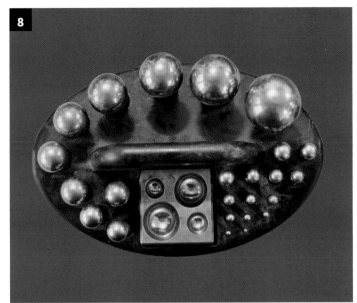

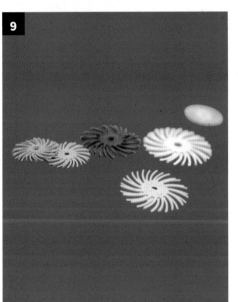

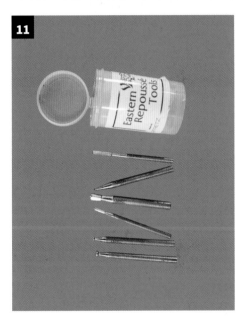

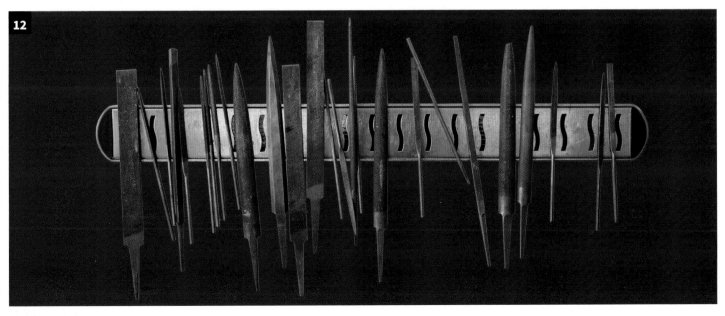

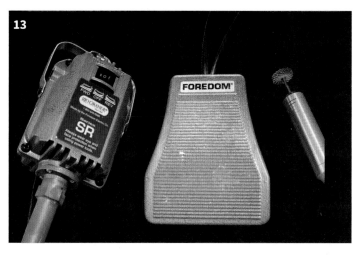

13

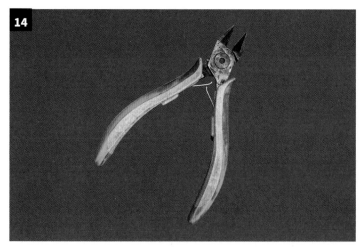

14

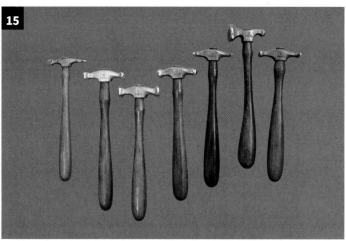

15

16

17A

17B

13. Flex shaft or high-speed Dremel Rotary Tool. A motorized machine designed to assist with drilling, cutting, carving, and polishing jewelry. The burs used with this tool are often used for cutting, carving, and setting gemstones; in this book, they are used for carving and sculpting metal.

14. Flush cutters. "Flush" refers to the shape of the jaws; any type of cutter can be "flush" if the jaws are beveled, creating a flat cut on one end of your wire and a V-shaped or pointed cut on the other.

15. Fretz hammer assortment. In addition to planishing and embossing hammers, the assortment includes raising hammers, which have rounded faces and are used in raising sheet metal.

16. GreenLion Saw Frame with saw blade. Also known as a piercing saw, a saw frame comprises a metal frame and handle that holds a fine saw blade using tension.

17. Mallet, rawhide or nylon. A soft striking tool designed to be used for working with soft metals; a rawhide mallet is made of tightly coiled leather.

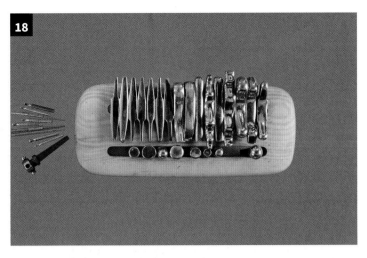

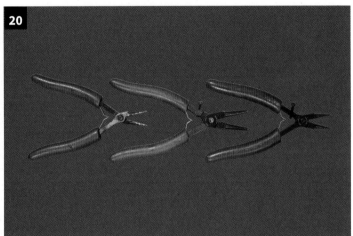

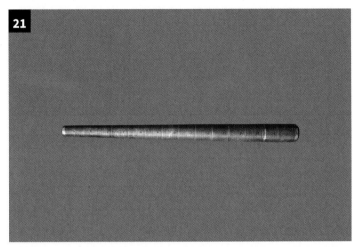

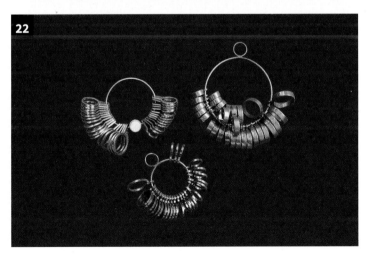

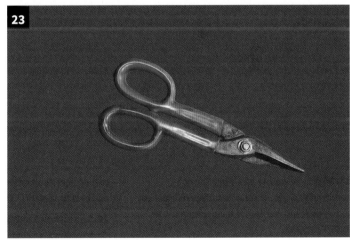

18. Miniature stake kit by Fretz. Designed by Bill Fretz, miniature stakes are specially created for smaller-scale shaping and forming such as rings, bezels and small vessels that can be difficult to make using full-sized stakes; the shapes and sizes of these stakes allow you to precisely shape smaller bezels for rings, bracelets, and pendants by stretching the metal to form curves, cups and rims.

19. Pickle pot.

20. Plier assortment. A pliers is a hand tool used to hold objects firmly.

21. Ring mandrel. A tapered tool, usually made from steel, that is used for forming, shaping and reshaping rings.

22. Ring sizers.

23. Shears.

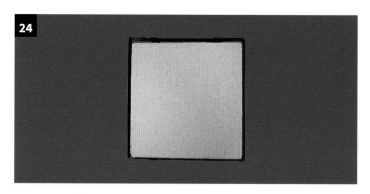

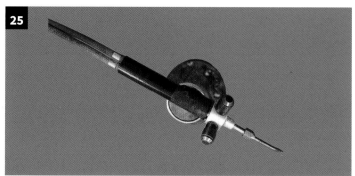

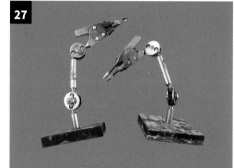

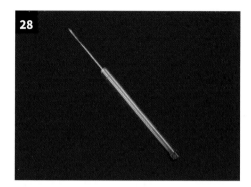

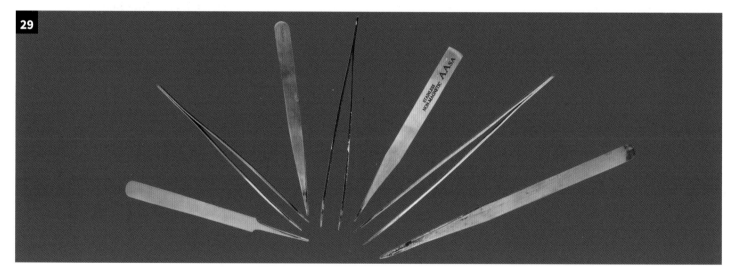

24. Silquar soldering platform. The non-combustible Silquar™ ceramic surface reflects heat to the work and withstands temperatures up to 2000°F (1093°C).

25. Smith Little Torch. Heating jewelry pieces during soldering is done with torches, which mix either oxygen or air with a gas such as butane, acetylene, or propane. The Smith Little Torch is a versatile Oxy-Fuel Torch, requiring both fuel (flammable gas), and Oxy (Oxygen) gas; also referred to as an Oxy-Propane, as Propane is the most popular fuel used with it. For a full discussion of the torch, its accompanying tools and supplies, and how to operate it, see page 27.

26. Swanstrom SawPlate System with Gary's Clamp. An aluminum SawPlate that promotes the precise position of your metal while improving ergonomics during sawing and piercing tasks. A replaceable plastic bearing surface ensures smooth rotation of the clamp and your work; locking screws secure the plate and clamp and your piece in place.

27. Third hand tool (also called a helping hand). Helps you easily position your work for hands-free soldering.

28. Titanium pick. A Titanium solder probe.

29. Tweezers.

A. *Precision tweezers.* Tweezers with fine tips that are tapered, beveled and very sharp, ideal for a variety of applications at the bench, including handling components and precisely placing small pieces of solder.

B. *Ti tweezers (titanium tweezers).* Made by Lion Punch Forge as an alternative to cross-locking tweezers; ideal for those with hand injuries or hand strength concerns. Used for soldering applications.

The Torch

To accomplish the majority of the tutorials in this book, you'll need one of the following torches. Small but mighty, they're my personal favorite.

1. Smith Little Torch Propane and Oxygen System
2. Smith Complete Little Torch Acetylene and Oxygen System
3. Smith Little Torch Propane Set with an oxygen concentrator

I have primarily used the Smith Little Torch Propane and Oxygen System since the beginning of my journey, so my instruction will focus entirely on that.

Smith Little Torch

Every torch needs oxygen for fuel to burn. In a basic torch, known as an *air-fuel* torch, the torch is connected directly to a gas cylinder, with the oxygen supplied by the air present in the atmosphere. Yet to achieve a more precise, hotter flame, additional oxygen is required. This can be achieved with a torch known as an oxy-fuel torch.

Both the Smith Little Torch Propane and Oxygen System and Smith Complete Little Torch Acetylene and Oxygen System are *oxy-fuel* torches that require both fuel and oxygen tanks. You may also see them referred to as an oxy-propane or oxy-acetylene torch.

The Smith Little Torch has a solid aluminum body combined with copper nozzles. It utilizes fine nozzles set with laser-drilled sapphires at its tips. The valves provide accurate control over flame size and temperature. It comes in a full color box containing the fully assembled torch with pre-attached hoses and brass connectors. The torch also comes with a set of five nozzles, also referred to as cutting tips, #3 to #7. The torch tips have center holes sized to deliver the proper amount of air and fuel gas at the proper pressure for a specific metal thickness.

Smith Little Torch Setup

Your torch must be connected to both fuel and oxygen. To do this, you need the following:

Oxygen cylinder. An oxygen storage vessel that is either held under pressure in gas cylinders.

Oxygen regulator. Reduces, controls, and measures the flow of oxygen to ensure a safe and effective working pressure.

Oxygen flashback arrestor. A safety device designed to stop a flame in its tracks.

Fuel gas cylinder. An DOT-approved portable container used for the transportation and storage of compressed gas.

Fuel gas regulator. A control device that maintains a defined pressure of a system by cutting off the flow of a gas or liquid when it reaches a set pressure

Fuel gas flashback arrestor. Designed to prevent the flame from flowing back to the hose and the regulator through the torch. All advanced flashback arrestors are equipped with check valves or coiled tubes that help prevent the reverse flow of gases.

You'll also need a flint striker or electronic igniter to light the torch safely.

Oxygen and Fuel

Before you purchase an oxy-fuel torch, be sure that you have access to fuel and oxygen cylinders from a local supplier, such as a welding supplier, builders' merchant, or gas supplier. Options might include monthly cylinder rental and payment for refills or buying a cylinder and swapping the empty for a full tank.

Oxygen is supplied as a compressed gas in steel cylinders ranging in size. It's smart to have a backup cylinder in case the first one runs out.

Some prefer to use acetylene, which burns at a much higher temperature than propane. It's important to note that acetylene is more volatile than propane. It can be more difficult to source and is generally more expensive.

I've chosen to use propane with my Smith Little Torch. I initially chose propane because my studio was situated inside my home and next to my daughter's room, and I was informed that propane was cleaner to breathe than any other fuel. I've continued to use propane because I find it easier on my eyes. Small propane cylinders are often readily available at gas stations or hardware stores, where they can also be refilled.

No matter which fuel you choose, be sure to check with your local fire department and insurance company to determine whether or not you can store them inside your workspace.

Regulators

Fine adjustments can be made by the valves on the torch itself to regulate the output pressure of the gas, but most of the work is done by the regulators connected to the top of the cylinder. Too much pressure and the flame will blow out. Too little and the flame won't generate enough heat.

Adjustable regulators ensure that the output pressure matches the gas you're utilizing. I recommend buying the regulators alongside your gas cylinders. Fixed propane regulators tend to provide too little pressure to be effective.

Dual-gauge regulators are ideal. A single-gauge regulator gives you a read on the output pressure. A dual-gauge regulator will also show you the input pressure so you can keep track of when the tank is nearing empty.

Flashback Arrestors

Flashback arrestors are brass tubes that attach to both gas hoses. With the pre-attached Smith Little Torch hoses, the flashback arrestors should be attached between the regulators and the hose. In the event of fire, the flashback arrestor cuts off the gas from that point onward.

Ignition

An igniter is an electro-explosive device (EED) that uses an externally applied electric current to produce a precisely controlled reaction of gas or flame for the initiation of a combustible compound.

Note. Using a cigarette lighter to ignite your torch is dangerous. **It's highly recommended to use the electronic, hands-free lighter specifically designed for torches.** [A]

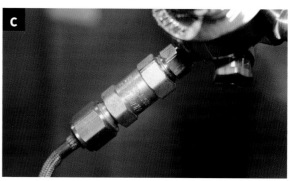

Connecting the Smith Little Torch

Even though they've invested in Smith Little Torches, many of my students continue to use their crème brûlée torches because they're daunted by the gas cylinders, potential fire hazards, and insurance coverage restrictions. However, if you follow the setup instructions, you'll find that they're much less intimidating than anticipated. Not only that, I promise you'll be thankful once you have your torch connected and ready to go. I've found the Smith Little Torch to be the most versatile torch on the market.

Regulators to the Fuel and Oxygen Cylinders

The fuel regulator is red in color and connects to the fuel cylinder with left-hand threads (counterclockwise), and the oxygen regulator is green and connects to the oxygen cylinder with right-hand threads (clockwise). To attach the regulators, screw the fuel regulator onto the fuel cylinder and the oxygen regulator onto the oxygen cylinder. [B]

Flashback Arrestors

Since on the Smith Little Torches the hoses are pre-attached, the flashback arrestors are connected directly to the regulators. The Smith Flashbacks Arrestor set contains two color-coded flashback arrestors: green for oxygen and red for fuel. Screw the flashback arrestors into the corresponding regulators. [C]

Hoses

Connect each of the Smith Little Torch hoses to the corresponding flashback arrestors: the green hoses are for the oxygen and the red are for the fuel. Note that each hose screws in the opposite direction: clockwise for oxygen and counterclockwise for fuel. (All US torch fittings are the standard "A" and "B" type fittings, which connect the torch to the hose and the hose to the regulators.)

Tighten all connections with a plumber's wrench. The fittings should be snug and airtight, but don't overdo it. All the gas fittings are made of brass, and the threads can easily become stripped with excessive force. [D]

Attach the Nozzles

The nozzles screw onto the end of the torch. Select the preferred nozzle (the number designating the torch nozzle size is stamped on the side) and screw it onto the end of the torch. Rotate the nozzle to the desired direction and tighten, finger-tight. [E]

Quick Check

If you suspect any leaks, check that the connectors are fully seated properly and tighten up with a wrench. If the fittings are screwed together correctly and straight, they should be airtight. Excessive force is not needed.

If you suspect a leak, spray the area with a detector spray and watch for small bubbles to appear. Tighten the connection and re-spray to check again.

Set the Pressure

Open the valves on the torch. Close the regulators and then open the gas cylinders. Adjust the regulators until the gauges show the desired output pressures. Close the torch valves.

This is how I set my regulators. If you look closely, the size of your torch tips are indicated with numbers (see photo E on page 29). Numbers #3, #4, and #5 should primarily be used with acetylene, and numbers #6 and #7 should primarily be used with propane. It's important to note that the output pressure (PSI) on your tanks should match the number of your torch tip. For instance, if I'm using a #6 tip on my Smith Little Torch, the output pressure on my regulator should read 6 PSI. [See photo F on page 29]

Operating the Torch

Here are my guidelines for the best way to use your Smith Little Torch.

1. Open the red gas valve on the torch one quarter turn. Ignite the gas. [A] Increase the gas for a larger flame.

2. Slowly open the green oxygen valve. As you increase the oxygen, the internal cone of the flame will turn a beautiful light blue. This is your soldering flame. [B] To increase the temperature, increase the gas first and then the oxygen. To decrease the temperature, decrease the oxygen first and then the

Scan to watch
a video tutorial

Holding the Torch

- I've seen many people hold their torches like a pencil. However, I recommend holding your torch in your fingers, with your palm facing down. The more sculptural your pieces become, the more versatile you'll find this way of holding the torch to be when trying to access hard-to-reach solder joints.

- Many traditional metalsmiths claim that torches should be held in nondominant hands so that precision work can be done using your dominant hand. I disagree. I recommend switching your torch back and forth between both hands. Determine what feels right and go with that, but know that the more ambidextrous you become, the more flexible you'll be when faced with different challenges.

gas. Either way, be sure to maintain the light blue internal cone.

Note. Too little oxygen will result in a flickering yellow flame. Too much oxygen will create a very sharp, lavender flame. If attempting to solder with too little oxygen, you'll find that you'll be watching and waiting, to no avail. Soldering using too much oxygen will burn off the flux, and the silver will oxidize before the solder has a chance to flow. [C, D]

3. For annealing, use more gas and less oxygen in order to gently warm the metal. If your flame is orange, which makes it difficult to determine the correct color and temperature, that is an indication that the torch tip is dirty. Use a brass brush to clean the tip. [E, F]

4. When you shut down your studio at the end of each day, you need to bleed, or flush, the hoses to ensure that they're filled with pure oxygen and gas. To do so, open the gas valve on the torch, ignite it, and allow the gas to escape until the flame dissipates. Close the gas valve. Open the oxygen valve to allow the oxygen to release. Close it once it's empty.

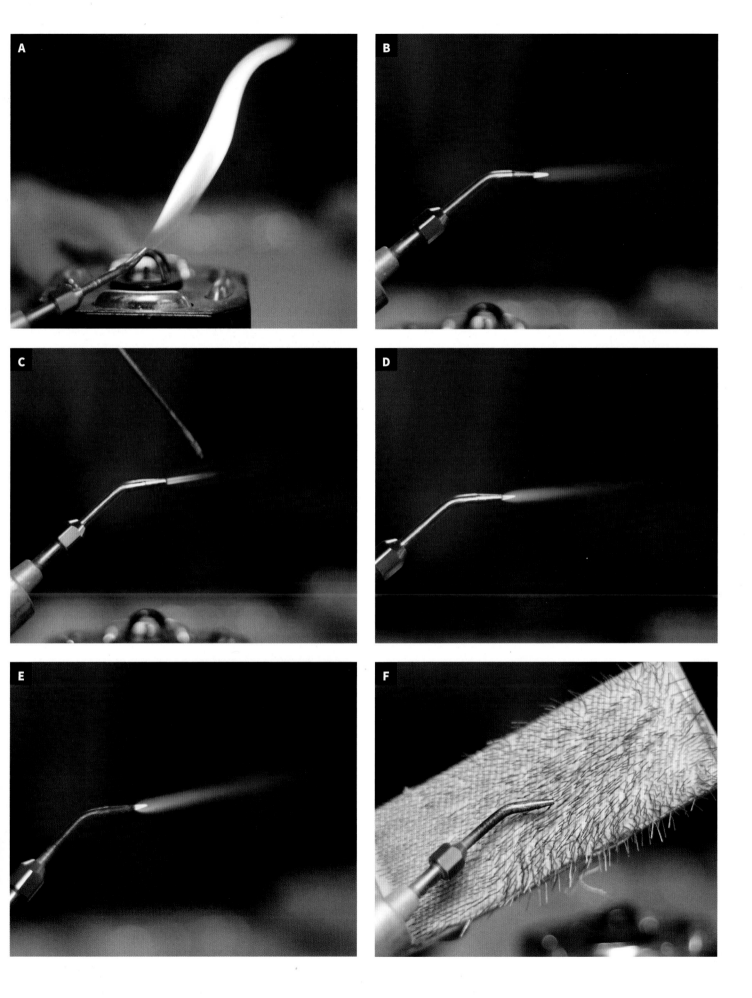

The
Projects

The First Challenge: Chains

I LIVE IN A REMOTE AREA OF WASHINGTON STATE, situated in the North Cascade Mountains, a mere 60 mile (97 km) jaunt on the Pacific Crest Trail toward Canada. Our home is one of nine homes on Lynx Lane, where we do see coyotes, cougars, black bears, moose, and the occasional lynx. When I purchased my first Smith Little Torch in 2011, there was no place close by that offered silversmithing classes. So for me, outside of the instructional video that arrived with the Smith Little Torch kit I purchased, it was baptism by fire.

In the beginning, I paged through jewelry catalogs, curious how specific textures, connections, and hinges were achieved. It was like solving an intricate puzzle. Looking back through photos of my first pieces, it's apparent that I was floundering. I sawed through thick sheet, breaking blade after blade, leaving edges rough and unpolished. My silver was covered with fire scale.

When I started offering workshops in 2017, I learned an extraordinary amount from my students. I'm embarrassed to admit that, at that time, I didn't know how important it was to neutralize pickle before disposing of it. In my defense, I did start with a homemade vinegar solution instead of purchasing sodium bisulphate. I had zero exposure to anyone using proper metalsmithing terminology, so I relied heavily on storytelling and comical body language to teach my self-discovered techniques. I wasn't familiar with extra easy, medium, and hard solder. Instead, I only used easy solder and taught myself how to use heat sinks to prevent previous solder joints from melting.

The most intriguing tidbit I learned from my students was that they had always been taught that it's simply not possible to fuse sterling silver. My response? "It isn't? I beg to differ."

Let me rewind six years.

I learned how to silversmith through a series of self-challenges. My first challenge was to make 100 chains. I contrived about 15 different designs that I repeated and augmented. To form links, I used pencils, butter knives, and crochet and knitting needles. I made a wire jig with scrap wood and nails to create decorative links. It wasn't until I'd made at least 50 chains that I purchased my first set of pliers.

If you're struggling with torch control, I encourage you to challenge yourself by making chains. The repetition of turning your torch on and off, up and down, and fusing and soldering small links is an excellent exercise that will undoubtedly help build upon your skill level.

The first chain I made was a standard round-link. I formed the rings around a pencil and snipped them apart with flush cutters. I soldered each and every ring and grew frustrated when the second, third, and fourth rings stuck to the solder from the first ring. I made a bigger mess when trying to reheat and separate the rings. It was then that I tried to fuse half of the jump rings first and only solder the middle (joining) ring. What a difference that made! Never again did I have problems with previous solder joints melting when making chains.

From that point onward, I only used easy solder for half of the round-link chain. All other chain links were fused, requiring no flux or solder.

This section comprises four different chain style tutorials, with a hook clasp tutorial included at the end.

Focusing on the Mass

It's important to always keep your "mass" in mind. No matter the size of your piece, the mass is the spot that contains the most silver. If you focus your torch on the most vulnerable points (the sides and tips) without heating the mass, you'll likely ball your wire or reticulate the edges of your silver. Instead, focus your torch on the mass.

BARBELLS

Tools and Materials

Smith Little Torch Propane and Oxygen System with #6 torch tip

Silquar Soldering Board

10'–15' (3 to 4.6 m) half-hard sterling silver wire, gauge 16

Half-hard sterling silver wire, gauge 18

Flush cutters

Round-nose pliers

Needle-nose pliers

Titanium pick

Copper tongs

Hammer

Anvil or steel bench block

Third hand tool

Flex shaft or high-speed Dremel Rotary Tool

Black silicone polishing disc

Techniques

Wire forming

Fusing sterling silver

Torch control

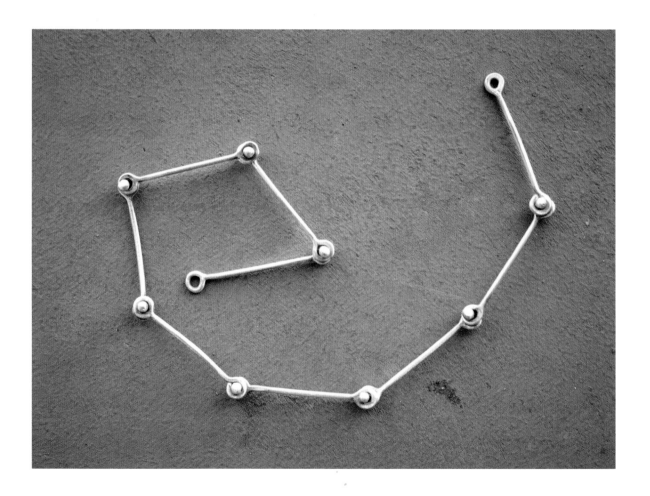

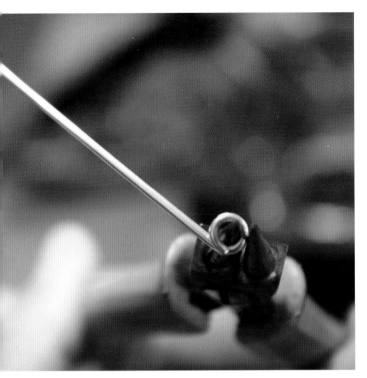

1. With flush cutters, snip the 16-gauge wire into 2-inch (5 cm) lengths. Play around with the length of the links to determine what kind of chain you prefer. I'll sometimes have longer links toward the front of a necklace with shorter ones at the back.

   On both ends, wrap the wire around round nose pliers to make two rings that resemble a barbell. Round nose pliers come in different sizes, so keep in mind that the rings should measure approximately 3 mm (⅛ inch) in diameter.

   Level the plane with needle-nose pliers. [A]

2. Before you begin to fuse, note the location of the mass. On the barbell chains, the mass is situated at the curve of the metal leading into the ring. The most vulnerable spot is the tip of the wire.

   Make sure you have your pick in hand.

   Your torch angle should be pointing straight down at the mass, not at an angle across the metal. [B]

   continued on next page

If the metal separates while you're heating the mass, use your pick to nudge it back into place. As soon as you see the silver fuse, you can move your torch to the center of the ring to "tighten" the fuse. You can use this method to shrink the ring if it's too big. Use your pick as a heat sink if you're worried that the ring will melt. [C]

3. Hammer all of the rings so that they're flat. This helps prevent the chain from kinking.

4. Snip the 18-gauge wire into ½-inch (1.3 cm) lengths. You should have one of these for every 2 barbell links.

5. One at a time, hold the 18-gauge wire in your copper tongs so that the wire is positioned perpendicular.

   Angle your torch sideways and heat the bottom tip of the wire. The wire will draw upwards into a ball. If the ball isn't perfectly smooth, you can fix that in step 9.

6. Place 2 barbell links together in the third hand. The rings should line up with one another and be positioned perpendicularly. Thread one of the balled 18-gauge wires through the 2 rings. [D]

7. Again, angle your torch sideways and heat the bottom tip of the wire until it draws upward into a ball. Repeat this step until your chain is the length you desire. [E]

8. With a flex shaft and black silicone polishing disc, sand down all sharp spots until the metal is consistently smooth to the touch.

Troubleshooting Tips

- If the 18-gauge wire drops off as you're melting it into a ball, that means you're attempting to heat too much of the wire. When you see the ball wiggle under the heat, it's indicating that it's struggling to hold its weight. STOP.

  However, if the weight did drop off and puddle on your soldering platform, hold the remaining wire in the middle of the dropped material. Focus your torch on both the dropped material and the end of the wire. It'll pull back into a ball.

- If the ball fuses to the bottom side of the barbell link, that means you have taken too long to heat the ball. Do not point your torch directly at the barbell links. Instead, turn up your torch, angle it sideways, and quickly heat it into a ball before it has a chance to fuse.

- If any of the ball rivets look disheveled, wait until the chain is complete. Then, lay the chain on the soldering platform with the disheveled ball facing up. One by one, angle your torch sideways and quickly heat only the surface of the ball until it's smooth.

  If the jump rings are too large for the ball rivets, you can either shrink the rings with your torch (step 3) or add more material. To do so, lay the chain on the soldering platform with the ball facing up. Place a tiny piece of scrap sterling silver on your soldering platform. Heat the scrap and while it's molten, sweep it up with your pick. As you angle your torch sideways, place your pick-with-scrap against the ball. Provided the scrap and ball are touching while you're heating both simultaneously, they will fuse into a larger ball rivet.

BICYCLE

Tools and Materials

Smith Little Torch Propane and Oxygen System with #6 torch tip

Silquar Soldering Board

20'–25' (6 to 7.6 m) half-hard sterling silver wire, gauge 16

Flush cutters

Round nose pliers

Needle-nose pliers

Straight nose pliers

Titanium pick

Copper tongs

Flex shaft or high-speed Dremel Rotary Tool

Black silicone polishing disc

Techniques

Wire forming

Fusing sterling silver

Torch control

1. With flush cutters, snip the 16-gauge wire into ¾- inch (2 cm) lengths.

2. On one end, wrap the wire around round-nose pliers to make one ring that resembles a lollipop. The rings should measure approximately ⅛ inch (3 mm) in diameter.

   Level the plane with needle-nose pliers so that the ring lays flat on the soldering platform. The seam doesn't need to be flush, but it must be touching.

3. Note the location of the mass. Just as with the barbell chain, the mass is situated at the curve of the metal leading into the ring. The most vulnerable spot is the tip of the wire.

   Make sure you have your pick in hand.

   Your torch angle should be pointing straight down at the mass, not at an angle across the metal.

   If the metal separates while you're heating the mass, use your pick to nudge it back into place. As soon as you see the silver fuse, move your torch to the center of the ring to tighten the fuse. [A, B]

4. You do not need to hammer the rings. One side will be rounded and the other flat from the soldering platform.

   With the flat side of the ring facing up in your needle-nose pliers, use the straight nose pliers to bend the wire into a 90-degree angle.

5. Set one link on your soldering platform with the ring lying flat and the tail facing skyward. Place the ring of a second link over the pin. [C]

continued on next page

6. Link by link, angle your torch sideways and quickly heat the pin until it slumps down into a ball. If the ball slumps toward the heat, you can switch your torch to the other side to even it out. Continue this step until your chain is the length you desire. [D]

7. With a flex shaft and black silicone polishing disc, sand down all sharp spots until the metal is consistently smooth to the touch.

Troubleshooting Tip

If the rings are too large for the ball rivets, you can either shrink the rings with your torch (step 3) or add more material:

1. Lay the chain on the soldering platform with the ball facing up.

2. Place a tiny piece of scrap sterling silver on your soldering platform. Heat the scrap and, while it's molten, sweep it up with your pick. [A, B]

3. As you angle your torch sideways, place your pick-with-scrap against the ball. [C] Provided the scrap and ball are touching while you're heating both simultaneously, they will fuse into a larger ball rivet. [D]

PADDLE

Tools and Materials

Smith Little Torch Propane and Oxygen System with #6 torch tip

Silquar Soldering Board

10'–15' (3 to 5 m) half-hard sterling silver wire, gauge 18

Round nose pliers or a knitting needle 2.5 mm in diameter (size 1.5)

Needle-nose pliers

Flush cutters

Titanium pick

Copper tongs

Hammer

Anvil or steel bench block

Flex shaft or high-speed Dremel Rotary Tool

Black silicone polishing disc

Techniques

Wire forming

Fusing sterling silver

Torch control

1. Wrap approximately ½ inch (1.3 cm) of 18-gauge wire around round-nose pliers or a knitting needle to create a coil. The rings should be 2.5 to 3 mm (approximately ⅛ inch) in diameter. [A]

2. With flush cutters, snip all the way through the coil so that you have a pile of individual jump rings.

   Straighten the rings out with needle-nose pliers so that they lay flat on the soldering platform, the seams touching but not necessarily flush.

3. Point the tip of your pick inside the jump ring and simultaneously heat the ring until it fuses.

   If the ring separates while you're heating, use your pick to nudge it back into place. As soon as you see the silver fuse, move your torch to the center of the ring to "tighten" the fuse. [B]

4. Hammer all the fused rings so that they are flat.

5. Snip the 18-gauge wire into 2-inch (5 cm) lengths. These should match the number of rings.

6. Lay the 2-inch (5 cm) pieces on your soldering platform. Heat one side of each piece until it balls (the top side will be rounded and the bottom be flat). [C]

7. Hammer the half round balls into flat paddles.

8. Thread one paddle link through rings 1 and 2.

   Set the piece on your soldering platform and heat the other side into a ball.

   Hammer it into a paddle.

9. Thread another paddle link through ring 2. Add ring 3. [D]

   Set the piece on your soldering platform and heat the other side into a ball. [E]

   Hammer it into a paddle.

10. Thread a third paddle link through ring 3. Add ring 4. Repeat these steps until the chain is the length you desire.

11. With a flex shaft and black silicone polishing disc, sand down all sharp spots until the metal is smooth to the touch.

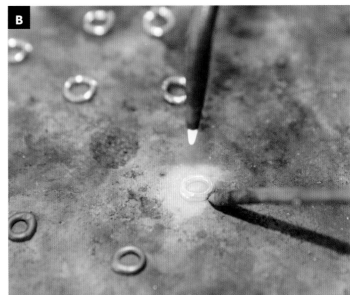

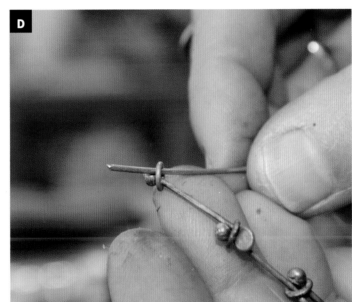

ROUND LINKS

Tools and Materials

Smith Little Torch Propane and Oxygen System with #6 torch tip

Silquar Soldering Board

10'–15' (3 to 5 m) half-hard sterling silver wire, gauge 18

Pencil or jump ring mandrel

Flush cutters

Needle-nose pliers

Titanium pick

Copper tongs

Third hand tool

My-T-Flux or similar liquid hard-soldering flux

Easy solder

Flex shaft or high-speed Dremel Rotary Tool

Black silicone polishing disc

Techniques

Wire forming

Fusing sterling silver

Pick soldering

Torch control

1. Wrap the 18-gauge wire around the pencil to create a coil. The rings should be 5 to 8 mm (approximately ⁵⁄₁₆-inch) in diameter. The smaller the rings, the longer it'll take to complete the chain. [A]

2. With flush cutters, snip all the way through the coil so that you have a pile of individual jump rings.

   Divide the jump rings in half. Set one half aside.

   Straighten the rings out with needle-nose pliers so that they lay flat on the soldering platform, the seams touching but not necessarily flush.

3. To ensure that the seam of each ring is touching, heat the back side of the ring (opposite the seam). As you do so, use your pick to nudge the opening closed. [B]

   Quickly move your torch to the opening of the jump ring, ensuring that you are heating both tips evenly until they fuse together. [C]

   Repeat this step until you've fused half the jump rings.

4. Place two fused jump rings onto one open jump ring. Without spreading the loop side to side, use two sets of pliers to close the opening until the points are touching.

continued on next page

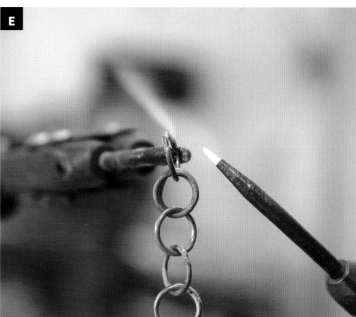

5. Set the unfused jump ring inside the third hand with the open seam facing up. The two fused jump rings should be dangling out of the way. Flux the seam.

   Note that the third hand functions as a heat sink. Therefore, try to position the ring so that the heat sinks evenly on both sides.

6. Put a piece of easy solder on your soldering platform. Heat the solder (not the pick) and as you pull your torch back, stick the tip of your pick into the solder to pick it up.

   If the solder smears across the soldering platform, your pick is either too hot or dirty.

7. Place the solder on the seam as you heat evenly between the two sides of the opening. [D, E]

   The solder will transfer from your pick to the silver when the silver is hot. Solder follows heat. If the solder drops off your pick, then you attempted the transfer before the silver was sufficiently hot.

   If the solder flows to the left, that means one of two things. You might be focusing your heat on the left side of the opening. Otherwise, the third hand might be sinking more heat on the right side of the ring. Either way, if this happens, you can heat the opposite side of the ring to coax the solder over.

8. Continue to add two fused rings to one open ring, flux, and solder. Repeat these steps until the chain is the length you desire. Pickle and quench.

9. With a flex shaft and black silicone polishing disc, sand down all sharp spots until the metal is smooth to the touch.

HOOK CLASP

Tools and Materials

Smith Little Torch Propane and Oxygen System with #6 torch tip

Silquar Soldering Board

2" (5 cm) Half-hard sterling silver wire, gauge 16

Round nose pliers

Needle-nose pliers

Titanium pick

Copper tongs

Hammer

Anvil or steel bench block

Flush cutters

Flex shaft or high-speed Dremel Rotary Tool

Black silicone polishing disc

Techniques

Wire forming

Fusing sterling silver

Torch control

---

1. On one end of the 16-gauge wire, wrap the wire around round-nose pliers to make one ring that resembles a lollipop.

Level the plane with needle-nose pliers so that the ring lays flat on the soldering platform. The seam doesn't need to be flush, but it must be touching. [A]

continued on next page

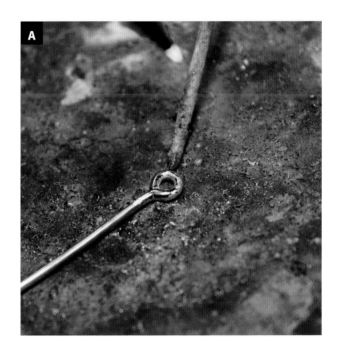

2. The mass is situated at the curve of the metal leading into the ring. The most vulnerable spot is the tip of the wire.

   Make sure you have your pick in hand.

   Your torch angle should be pointing straight down at the mass, not at an angle across the metal.

   If the metal separates while you're heating the mass, use your pick to nudge it back into place. As soon as you see the silver fuse, move your torch to the center of the ring to tighten the fuse.

3. Hammer the ring flat.

4. Bend the shaft around your pick. You can roll it back and forth until the hook is the size you want. [B]

   With flush cutters, snip the point of the hook and use round nose pliers to bend the throat, which helps guide the hook into the jump ring. [C]

5. Hammer to work-harden the bend. [D]

6. With a flex shaft and black silicone polishing disc, sand down all sharp spots until the metal is smooth to the touch.

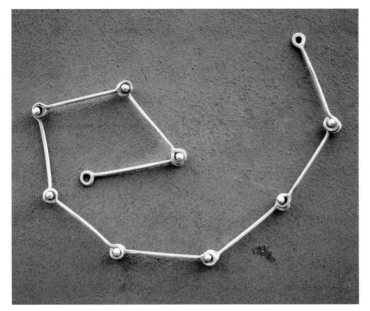

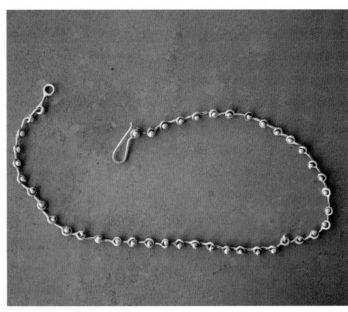

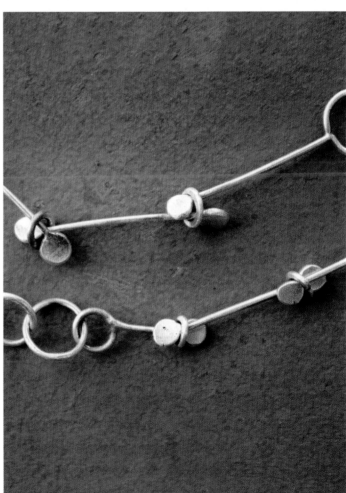

The Second Challenge: Hand-Fabricated Botanicals

DURING THE THREE MONTHS THAT I CHALLENGED MYSELF TO FABRICATE BOTANICALS, I literally dissected and studied thirty different plants. I marveled at how things grew from embryonic shoot to leaf, from bud to bloom, and how nodding pink spring Prairie Smoke flowers could give rise to feathery, smoky-pink seed heads. I spent countless minutes staring at each plant, considering the steps I might take to re-create each precious detail in silver.

I glued leaves and petals onto silver sheet to saw around the shapes. I experimented with hammers, nails, and awls to explore textures, even spending a considerable amount of time on the floor pounding annealed metal against concrete, wood, stones, and other rough surfaces. I was elated with each discovery. I snapped black and white photographs of each live specimen as well as my own tests on silver and when it was difficult to tell the difference between the two pictures, I was ecstatic.

The most mystifying portion of the puzzle was, once each component was ready, figuring out how to reassemble without melting them and create lifelike, wearable sculptures. In this scenario, baptism by fire isn't just a metaphor. I made countless mistakes, walked away from my bench more times that I could count, yet pushed through every single project until I had, at the very least, learned from my efforts.

The following three tutorials will give you an idea as to how my brain worked as I first started my journey into silver botanical fabrication.

LEAF

Tools and Materials

Smith Little Torch Propane and Oxygen System with #6 torch tip

Silquar Soldering Board

Sterling silver sheet, gauge 22 (for a pendant) or 24 (for earrings)

Both 16- and 21-gauge sterling silver wire

Rubber cement (optional)

GreenLion Saw Frame

2/0 or 3/0 saw blades

Bench pin

Flush cutters

Separating disc

My-T-Flux or similar liquid hard-soldering flux

Easy solder

Titanium pick

Copper tongs

Black silicone polishing disc

Flex shaft or high-speed Dremel Rotary Tool

Eastern Repoussé and Chasing Tools Set

Fretz Chasing Hammer

Anvil or steel bench block

Round nose pliers

Fiber wheels, fine and coarse

Techniques

Sawing

Soldering wire horizontal to sheet

Sweat soldering

Forming sheet between wire

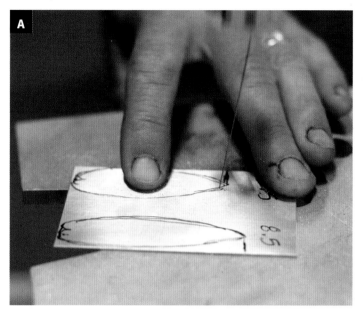

1. To transfer the image of a leaf to the silver sheet, I either print out the picture, trace an image on my phone, or use an actual leaf to glue onto silver sheet.

2. Saw out the shape. Remember to continue your sawing motion through the curves so that you don't break your blade. [A]

3. When I've finished sawing out the leaf shape, I anneal my silver, a foolproof way of cleaning it. Use a softer flame to anneal and watch for the silver to turn black when you draw your torch away from it. Pickle. [B]

4. In the meantime, with flush cutters, snip one length of 16-gauge wire for the center vein and several lengths of 21-gauge for the side veins.

5. Taper one end of the 16-gauge wire using the separating disc. [C]

6. When the leaf is white in the pickle, rinse, and dry.

7. Place the 16-gauge wire down the center of the leaf. Flux the entire leaf.

8. Place 3 small pieces of easy solder alongside the wire. [D]

9. Heat the wire directly across from each solder bit. This way, you'll draw the solder up so that it puddles on the wire. As soon as it does, move to the next solder bit. This technique will prevent the solder from puddling onto the sheet, which translates to less clean up. [E]

10. Turn up your torch and focus the heat on the mass (the sheet), not the wire, until your solder runs the entire length beneath the wire. You may need to apply slight pressure on your wire with your pick because the solder will not run if there's a gap. You can also use your pick as a heat sink to prevent the tip of the wire from balling. Pickle. [F, G, H]

continued on next spread

Scan to watch
a video tutorial

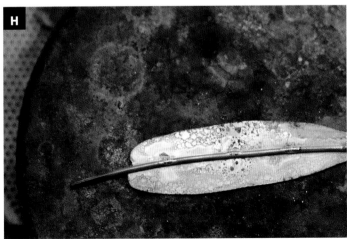

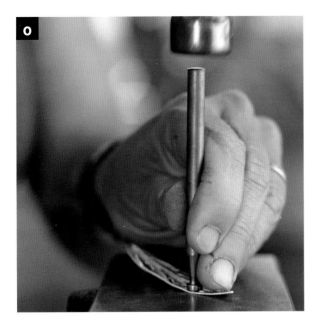

Scan to watch a video tutorial

11. Rinse, dry, and add the 21-gauge side veins. Flux. [I]

12. Place one small piece of easy solder next to each vein.

13. Again, with the heat of your torch, draw the solder up onto the wire one at a time.

14. Turn up your torch and focus on heating the mass below the wire.

15. Once the solder runs beneath each side vein, turn up your torch once more and focus the heat on the center vein while simultaneously nudging the side veins with your pick. This creates a seamless connection between the veins that you won't have to file later. Pickle until it's white. [J, K]

16. Snip off the excess wire.

17. Use the black silicone polishing disc to sand down the rough edges of the veins until they are flush with the sheet. [L]

18. With the repoussé chasing tools, begin with a line tool to add form to the tight spots between the veins, swiveling the back and forth without lifting the tool. [M]

    Note. To create a more pronounced form, try experimenting with a rubber block or sandbag instead of your anvil. I generally use my pinky to hold my piece steady, but if you prefer, you can tape it down to the surface.

19. With the small planishing tool, add form alongside the wire. As you hammer, drag the tool rather than lift. Finally, switch to the larger planishing tool on the outer edges of the leaf. [N, O]

    Note. As you add form or texture to the leaf, it'll turn gray and hard. To continue to work the metal, you'll need to anneal it so that it doesn't become too brittle and crack.

20. Once you're happy with the form or texture, re-anneal. Use round nose pliers to twist the metal slightly to give it an organic shape.

21. Use the separating disc to taper the boxy edges of the silver sheet, making the silver appear more organic.

22. Use the black silicone polishing disc to soften the edges.

23. I usually oxidize my pieces. I give them a final polish with an assortment of fiber wheels.

DANDELION

Tools and Materials

Smith Little Torch Propane and Oxygen System with #6 torch tip

Silquar Soldering Board

Sterling silver sheet, gauge 22

18-gauge sterling silver round wire

16-gauge sterling silver round wire

Flush cutters

Titanium pick

Copper tongs

My-T-Flux or similar liquid hard-soldering flux

Easy, medium, and hard solder

GreenLion Saw Frame

2/0 saw blade

Bench pin

Fretz HMR-12 Sharp Texturing/ Raising Hammer

Separating disc

Black silicone polishing disc

Flex shaft or high-speed Dremel Rotary Tool

Drill bits for size 16-gauge wire

Third hand tool

Assortment of pliers

Techniques

Fusing wire

Sawing

Texturing sheet with hammers

Piercing

Soldering multiple layers onto wire

1. With flush cutters, snip twenty-four ¼-inch (6 mm) lengths of 18-gauge wire to lay out in the following star formations: 3, 5, 7, and 9.

2. Make sure each piece of wire is touching at the center. Pay attention to the angle of your torch. To fuse, each piece of wire must come to the red fusing point at the exact same time. If one piece of wire balls, use your pick to nudge it inward, into the center of the mass. [A, B]

3. Flux each fused star and sweat hard solder to each center. Pickle, quench, and set aside. [C]

4. Using the 22-gauge sheet, saw out two flower patterns. Anneal, pickle, and quench.

5. Use a Fretz HMR-12 Sharp Texturing/Raising Hammer to add lined texture along the petals. Be sure to hammer consistently across each petal to ensure that it looks organic.

6. File down and soften the edges of the petals with a separating disc followed by the black silicone polishing disc. Pickle, quench, and set aside.

7. Using the flex shaft and drill bit for 16-gauge wire, drill a hole through the center of each star and flower formation. The 3-pointed star is the only one that does NOT need to be drilled.

8. Snip a piece of 16-gauge wire, approximately 2 inches (5 cm) in length.

continued on next page

9. Hold the 16-gauge wire in your third hand vertical, with one end sitting on top of the 3-pointed star. Flux.

   Use hard solder to join these two. [D, E]

10. Bend the 3-pointed star forward and place it in your third hand right at the solder joint. The third hand will act as a heat sink.

    Focus your torch on the tip of each wire until it balls.

11. Feed the 5-pointed star onto the wire. Ensure that there is no gap between the layers. The piece should be sitting upside down on your soldering platform to protect the weight from dropping off as you solder the second layer. Hold the wire with the third hand, but be sure it's not adding weight to your piece. Otherwise, as you heat, the wire may snap apart. Flux the entire piece.

    Heat the entire mass. Watch for the metal to turn yellow. Sweat medium solder to the wire. To do so, heat the entire piece until the metal begins to turn yellow. Then, change the angle of your torch so that you're heating the wire and not the mass. Continue heating until the solder puddles on the wire. Once it does, turn your torch downward to the mass to draw the solder from the wire down into the hole. Pickle and quench. [G]

12. Bend the 5-pointed star forward and place it in your third hand, right at the solder joint.

    Focus your torch on the tip of each wire until it balls. [H]

13. Feed the 7-pointed star onto the wire and repeat every instruction in step 10, using easy solder. Repeat step 11.

14. Feed the 9-pointed star onto the wire and repeat every instruction in step 10, using easy solder. Repeat step 11. Repeat these steps as you add the final 2 layers of flower petals. [I, J]

15. Using pliers, twist the petals to make them more realistic. [K]

16. Use the black silicone polishing disc to soften the edges and get rid of any sharp spots. Finish as desired.

ACORN

Tools and Materials

Smith Little Torch Propane and Oxygen System with #6 torch tip

Silquar Soldering Board

Both 24- and 22-gauge sterling silver sheet

1" (2.5 cm) 18-gauge sterling silver wire

Disc cutter

Brass hammer

Anvil or steel bench block

GreenLion Saw Frame

2/0 and 3/0 saw blades

Bench pin

File or separating disc

Titanium pick

Copper tongs

Hard, medium, and easy solder

My-T-Flux or similar liquid hard-soldering flux

Dapping set with block

Awl

Drill bit for 18-gauge wire

Sandpaper

Third hand tool

Flush cutters

Bale (optional)

Black silicone polishing disc

Flex shaft or high-speed Dremel Rotary Tool

Techniques

Sawing

Soldering multiple layers of sheet together

Forming with dapping block

Elongating form with dapping block

Pick soldering

Soldering together hollow form

Closing hollow form pinhole

Soldering to closed hollow form (optional)

1. If you would like to make this a MUCH simpler process, you do not need to layer the acorn cupule (the cup-shaped base of the acorn). Instead, you can simply cut out one circle and texture it with either your hammers or flex shaft and call it good. However, should you prefer the more complicated route, follow along with steps 2 through 9.

2. For the acorn cupule, with 24-gauge sheet, cut out TWO 1-inch (2.5 cm) circles and ONE of each of the following: ⅞ inch (2.2 cm), ¾ inch (2 cm), ⅝ inch (1.6 cm), ½ inch (1.3 cm), ⅜ inch (1 cm), and ¼ inch (6 mm). [A]

3. For the acorn nut, using 22-gauge sheet, cut out one 1-inch (3 cm) circle. Anneal, pickle, and quench. [B]

4. Take the smallest circle, the ¼-inch (0.6 cm) circle, and saw it into the shape of a star. Be sure not to shorten the tips of the star as you're sawing. Even out your saw lines with a file or separating disc. [C]

5. Sweat solder easy solder onto the back side of the ¼-inch (6 mm) star. Pickle and quench. Place it on top of the ⅜-inch (1 cm) circle. Flux and heat them until they are soldered together.

Note. If you prefer to heat your piece from below as shown, be sure to flux both the top and bottom. Once the solder has run, pickle and quench. [D]

continued on next page

6. Saw a star out of the ⅜-inch (1 cm) circle, this time ensuring that the points land halfway between the points of the ¼-inch (6 mm) star.

   Sweat easy solder to the back side and pickle.

   Continue this process until you have soldered together 7 of the circles and saw them into star shapes, using only one of the 1-inch (2.5 cm) 24-gauge circles.

7. Finally, solder together the first 7 stars to the second 24-gauge 1-inch (2.5 cm) circle. Do not saw that one out. You should have 7 layers of stars sitting on top of a circle, all soldered together. Anneal, pickle, and quench.

   At this point, you should have a flat cupule and one remaining 1-inch (2.5 cm) 22-gauge circle. [E]

8. Dap the 8-layer cupule. Begin with the largest possible cup size, working your way consecutively to smaller cups. [F]

   Once the edge of the cupule sits above the dapping block cup, you'll need to alter your technique.

   Tilt the cupule so that as you dap, you'll be hitting the sides in order to avoid marring the metal. Hammer the dapping punch straight downward, rotating the cupule until the entire circumference fits within the cup. [G]

   Replace the cupule to its original position so that sits straight inside the cup. Hammer directly downward.

9. Repeat step 8 once more. Then, place the cupule back in a wider cup and use a larger dapping punch to splay and flatten any kinks. Pickle, quench, and set it aside.

10. With the 22-gauge 1-inch (2.5 cm) circle, repeat steps 8 and 9 twice for the acorn nut. The goal is for the acorn nut to fit snugly inside the cupule. [H]

    Make note of the color of the silver as you dap. If it becomes gray and hard, you'll need to re-anneal before you continue.

11. As stated above, the acorn nut should fit snugly within the cupule. Now, your goal is to lengthen the form. To do so, refrain from hammering the edge. As you move to smaller and smaller cups, you'll still tilt the form as much as possible, but leave the edge alone. [I]

12. Place the nut into the smallest dapping cup and instead of a dapping punch, hammer the awl into the center to create the remains of the style (the pointed tip). [J]

13. With the drill bit to fit 18-gauge wire, drill a hole through the point. A pinhole is essential to prevent your hollow form from exploding when heated. Anneal, pickle, and quench. [K]

14. Sand down the edges of both cups to ensure that there are no air pockets when nestled together.

15. Place the cupule upside down on your soldering platform. Place the nut on top, ensuring that the connection is flush all the way around.

    Set 5 to 6 pieces of hard solder along the rim of the cap. Flux. [L]

    continued on next spread

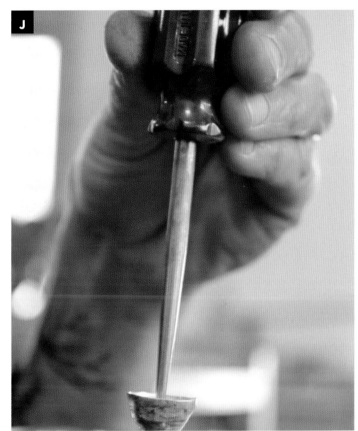

16. Heat the entire piece, focusing more time on the cupule to draw the solder in and downward. The solder MUST flow the entire way around the seam. [M]

17. If you think there might be a gap, wait until your piece cools. Gently hammer the cupule to ensure that snugly cups the nut. Re-flux and repeat step 15. [N]

18. If you're confident that your seam is securely soldered, you can close the pinhole. To do so, place 18-gauge wire into the pinhole. Hold the wire steady with the third hand.

19. Sweat medium solder to the wire. Heat the entire piece until the metal begins to turn yellow. Change the angle of your torch so that you're heating the wire and not the mass (the acorn). Continue heating until the solder puddles on the wire. Once it does, turn your torch downward to the mass to draw the solder from the wire down into the hole. [O, P]

   Note. You do not want to heat a closed form if there is an air pocket because when heated, it will explode. If you're concerned that your acorn has an air pocket, you can test it by gently hammering the edges to see if the solder seams pop open. If it's securely soldered, you can pickle and quench.

20. With flush cutters, snip off the excess wire, leaving just a small point. [Q]

21. To add a bale, sweat solder easy solder to the tip of the bale. Hold the bale against the acorn with a third hand. Heat the mass to coax the solder from the bale. I like to create a bale that resembles a stalk. This technique will be covered in the Branches project on page 86. [R]

22. Pickle and quench. Snip off the excess 18-gauge wire. Remove sharp spots with the black silicone polishing disc. Finish as desired.

Scan to watch
a video tutorial

Mature Poppy Seedpod

The following instructions will guide you through my own first poppy pod creation, which have advanced to now include intricate pores, a baby rattle, and hinged seed box. There are many different ways of fabricating a hollow form poppy pod, some of which can be quite complex, such as including the open valves allowing for seed dispersal.

After your first endeavor, I encourage you to take this tutorial one step further and see where your own explorations take you.

Tools and Materials

Smith Little Torch Propane and Oxygen System with #6 torch tip

Silquar Soldering Board

Sterling silver sheet, gauge 22

1' (30 cm) 21-gauge sterling silver wire

4" (10 cm) 16-gauge sterling silver wire

3" (7.6 cm) 12-gauge sterling silver wire

Disc cutter

Brass hammer

Anvil or steel bench block

Flush cutters

Titanium pick

Copper tongs

My-T-Flux or similar liquid hard-soldering flux

Easy, medium, and hard solder

Rawhide mallet (optional)

Separating disc

Black silicone polishing disc

Dapping set with block

Third hand tool

Sandpaper

Drill bit for 16-gauge wire

Carbide cone bur

Flex shaft or high-speed Dremel Rotary Tool

Eastern Repoussé and Chasing Tools Set

Fretz Chasing Hammer

Anvil or steel bench block

Cross locking tweezers

Stainless steel locking head and shank tweezers (optional)

Stainless steel binding wire (optional)

Techniques

Fusing wire

Sweat soldering

Forming with dapping block

Pick soldering

Soldering together hollow form

Closing hollow form pinhole

Light carving and texturing with flex shaft

Soldering to closed hollow form (optional)

1. With the disc cutter, cut out two 1-inch (2.5 cm) discs and one ¾-inch (2 cm) disc. Anneal, pickle, quench, and set aside. [A]

2. Begin by making the poppy crown. With flush cutters, snip the 21-gauge wire into fourteen ¼-inch (6 mm) lengths. Place them in a star-shaped pattern on your soldering platform and ensure that each point is touching at the center. [B]

3. For this particular step, it's important for you to keep your pick in hand, and torch angle is key. You will be fusing, so no flux or solder is required. Point your torch directly downward and into the center of the wires. Watch carefully to ensure that each wire is still touching and turns molten at the exact same time. If one wire disconnects from the mass and balls up, use your pick to nudge it inward toward the center of the mass. Provided the angle of your torch is accurate, all 10 wires should fuse to one another at the center. Pickle and quench. [C, D]

continued on next page

4. Turn the fused star upside down. Flux and sweat a few pieces of hard solder to the bottom. Pickle and quench. [E, F]

5. Place the star solder-side down on top of the ¾-inch (1 inch) disc. If the wires are not flush against the disc, gently hammer them down with a rawhide mallet. Flux.

   Note. If you're soldering these two layers from below, you'll need to flux both the top and underneath. Heat until the solder reflows. Pickle and quench. Snip off any excess wire. [G, H]

6. Between each wire on the poppy cap, use the separating disc to create the stigmatic rays (notches). [I]

7. Use the separating disc and then the black silicone polishing disc to blend the wire into the back plate as well as taper and smooth the edges of the crown. [J]

8. Place the crown face up inside a dapping cup and dap until the cap is lightly concave. [K]

9. Place the crown face down on your soldering platform. Place the wire in the third hand so that it's resting flush against the center of the crown. [L]

   Flux. Sweat hard solder to the wire. Heat the entire piece until the metal begins to turn yellow. Then, change the angle of your torch so that you're heating the wire and not the mass (the crown). Continue heating until the solder puddles on the wire. Once it does, turn your torch downward to the mass to draw the solder from the wire down into the hole. Pickle and quench. Set the cap aside.

   continued on next spread

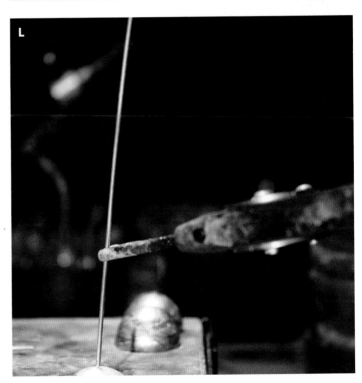

10. At this point, you'll make the capsule. Dap both of the 1-inch (2.5 cm) discs. Begin with the largest possible cup size, working your way consecutively to smaller cups.

Once the edge of each disc sits above the dapping block cup, tilt it so that, as you dap, you'll be hitting the sides in order to avoid marring the metal. Hammer the dapping punch straight downward, rotating the disc until the entire circumference fits within the cup. [M]

Replace the disc to its original position so that sits straight inside the cup. Hammer directly downward. Your goal is to form a perfect round sphere. [N]

11. Sand the edges of each cup until when held together, there are no gaps. The seam must be perfectly flush all the way around. Anneal, pickle, and quench. [O]

12. Drill a hole into the center of one of the cups. [P]

13. Pick and sweat hard solder along the edge of the cup with the hole. For this technique, make sure that your pick is clean and silver fluxed. Place 6 to 8 pieces of hard solder on your soldering platform. Heat the solder, not your pick. Immediately after the solder balls, pull your torch back and sweep the solder up with your pick. Heat the cup until it turns yellow and one by one, transfer each piece of solder to the rim of the cup, placing them approximately ⅛ inch (3 mm) apart. [Q]

Turn your torch down to heat the inside of the cup so that the solder sweats on the inside rather than outside the rim (there will be less solder to clean up this way).

continued on next spread

14. For this next step, I like to use a damaged Silquar Soldering Board to balance the sphere. Other options are to use stainless steel locking head and shank tweezers or a nest of binding wire. If you're choosing my method, set the cup without the hole in a cavity in your soldering platform. Balance the cup with the solder and hole on top. Flux. Check to make sure the seam is flush all the way around. [T]

It helps to secure the sphere by holding your pick on the top next to the hole until the flux has foamed. [U]

Heat the entire sphere, focusing a little more on the bottom cup to coax the solder downward. The solder should run all the way around the seam.

If there is an air pocket in your first attempt at solder flow, wait until the sphere cools to room temperature. Re-flux. Pick solder an additional piece of hard solder to the outside of the seam.

Do not pickle or quench. Wait for the capsule to cool to room temperature. Use sandpaper to grind off excess solder and conceal the seam.

15. Drill through the first hole and all the way through the opposite side of the capsule. Your capsule should now have two holes that line up.

16. Stick the 16-gauge wire through both holes of the capsule so that the crown is sitting flush on one side of the sphere. Then, hold the wire in the third hand with the poppy pod sitting upright on top of the third hand. Check to make sure the crown is still flush with the capsule. Flux. [V]

17. Place 1 to 2 pieces of medium solder on your soldering platform. Heat the entire mass until it begins to turn yellow. Pick and sweat medium solder to the underside of the crown right where it meets the capsule. Once the solder has adhered to that spot, move your torch to the opposite side of the joint to draw the solder through. By doing so, you should be filling the hole.

If you do not feel confident that the hole is closed, repeat this step.

Do not pickle or quench. Wait until your piece has cooled to room temperature.

18. Turn the poppy pod upside down to rest on the soldering platform. Hold the wire with the third hand. Be sure it's not adding weight to your piece. Flux the whole pod.

Heat the mass. Watch for the metal to turn yellow. At that moment, sweat easy solder to stem, just above hole. Turn your torch downward to the mass to draw the solder from the wire down into the hole. At this point, you can pickle and quench.

19. At this point, you'll fabricate the pedicel. Hold the 12-gauge wire with cross locking tweezers so that one end is resting on your soldering platform. Direct your torch at that end and without placing extra pressure on the wire, heat it until it slumps. Pickle and quench.

The pedicel will provide a convenient handle for you to hold onto for step 20. [W, X]

20. To create the striations in a mature seedpod, you can use a variety of bits in your flex shaft, including shaving off some of the silver using a carbide cone bur. Use a rag to clean the capsule but refrain from placing it in the pickle or quench. [Y, Z]

21. To accentuate the striations, use a hammer and the small planishing tool to gently slope each striation inward. This is an excellent way to test whether or not your seams are 100% soldered shut because if not, they will pop open. [AA]

continued on next spread

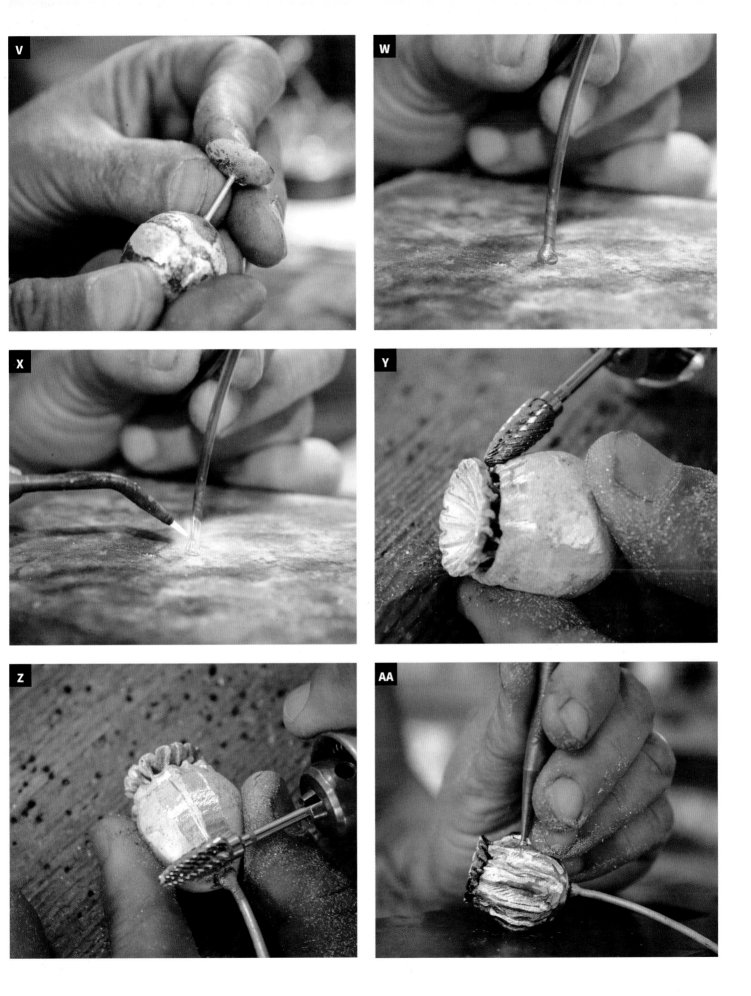

22. Snip off the excess 16-gauge wire from your poppy pod.

Set the poppy pod upside down to rest on the soldering platform. Place the slumped 12-gauge wire flush with the bottom of the capsule (where the wire was snipped). Place easy solder inside, making sure that it's touching the inside wall of the tube. Flux the whole pod, including the tube.

Heat the entire mass. Watch for the metal to turn yellow. Angle your torch toward the capsule, rotating around the outer edge of the wire. Watch for the solder to flow into the seam. Pickle and quench. [BB, CC]

23. Remove sharp spots with the separating disc and the black silicone polishing disc. Finish as desired. [DD]

FROM POPPY POD TO BLOSSOM

Tools and Materials

Sterling silver sheet, gauge 22

A torch, pick, tongs, flux, etc.

Size #6 torch tip

Soldering platform

Third hand

Easy solder

Saw frame

2/0 saw blades

Bench pin

Flex shaft

A separating disc

Black silicone polishing disc

Drill bit for 16-gauge wire

#12 Fretz Raising Hammer

Steel bench block or anvil

Round nose pliers

Techniques

Sawing

Texturing with hammer

Pick soldering

1. If you choose to transform your poppy pod into a blossom, you will maintain the 16-gauge wire and omit the step to fabricate a pedicel.

2. Repeat step 1 from the dandelion tutorial changing the length of the star formations from ¼ inch to ½ inch (6.4 mm to 13 mm). Snip twenty (or more if you're up for the challenge) ½-inch (13 mm) lengths of 18-gauge wire to lay out in two star-shape formations.

3. Repeat steps 2 and 3 from the Dandelion tutorial (see page 59).

4. One star shape at a time, repeat steps 10 and 11 from the Dandelion tutorial, feeding the stars onto the wire on the underside of the poppy pod, this time only using easy solder to close the pinholes. Once all layers are soldered in place, ball the end of each wire. Pickle, quench, and set aside.

5. To obtain the shape of the petals I usually print out a template or use actual poppy petals to glue onto the 22-gauge sterling silver sheet. Paste 2 sets of 2 petals onto the sheet mirror-facing so that they both look like an hourglass. Saw out the shapes, leaving enough room at the center of each pair of petals to drill your hole. Anneal, pickle, and quench.

6. With the #12 Fretz raising hammer, very consistently hammer lines from the center outward. The repetitive hammering will texture and form the petals. It will also expand the silver. Watch the color for hardness, as you may need to anneal to prevent tearing the metal.

7. Use the separating disc to continue the textured lines to the very edge of the petals. In this manner you will also be tapering the edges. Gently twist the petals with round nose pliers to give them more movement, and soften the edges with a black silicone disc.

8. Just as you did with the dandelion, add the petal layers onto the wire and, one at a time, repeat step 10. You will need to pay special attention to the colors of the silver because, with more mass, it will take longer to bring the solder to a melting point.

9. Finish as desired.

String of Pearls Succulent

In addition to the previously noted benefits of practicing chain making, many components of the chain designs covered earlier can be incorporated into fabricating botanicals. In the Luna Moth project (see page 142), we delve further into kinetics, but for now, you'll understand how a simple barbell chain can transform a string of pearls succulent into cascading tendrils.

This tutorial will guide you through the making of a three-strand string of pearls pendant. I often merge it with the barbell chain, but of course, you may alter the steps to make a pair of earrings or choose a different necklace design.

Tools and Materials

Smith Little Torch Propane and Oxygen System with #6 torch tip

Silquar Soldering Board

22-gauge sterling silver sheet

18- and 16-gauge sterling silver wire

Disc cutter

Brass hammer

Anvil or steel bench block

Dapping set with block

Awl

Drill bits for 18- and 16-gauge wire

Sandpaper

Hard, medium, and easy solder

My-T-Flux or similar liquid hard-soldering flux

Titanium pick

Copper tongs

Third hand tool

Flush cutters

Black silicone polishing disc

Flex shaft or high-speed Dremel Rotary Tool

Cross locking tweezers

Stainless steel binding wire (optional)

Techniques

Fusing wire

Forming with dapping block

Pick soldering

Sweat soldering

Soldering together hollow form

Closing hollow form pinhole

Soldering multiple joints onto a single wire

The benefit of heat sinks

Ball rivets

1. With the disc cutter, cut out an even number of discs with each of the following punches: 6 mm (¼ inch) and 10 mm (⅓ inch).

   A string of pearls succulent can be very time consuming. The number of discs you cut depends on how many pearls you want to include in your piece. As a reference, to make 2-strand string of pearls earrings, I usually fabricate 10 to 12 pearls per strand, graduating from small to big, which breaks down to this:

   - 12 small pearls = twenty-four 6 mm (¼-inch) discs

   - 12 large pearls = twenty-four 10 mm (⅓-inch) discs

2. Anneal the discs. Pickle and quench. [A]

3. Dap all of the discs. For each disc, begin with the largest possible cup size, working your way consecutively to smaller cups.

Once the edge of each disc sits above the dapping block cup, tilt it so that, as you dap, you'll be hitting the sides in order to avoid marring the metal. Hammer the dapping punch straight downward, rotating the disc until the entire circumference fits within the cup.

Replace the disc to its original position so that sits straight inside the cup. Hammer directly downward. Your goal is to form a perfect round sphere. [B]

4. Place one half of the cups into the smallest dapping cup and instead of a dapping punch, hammer the awl into the center to create the nib. [C, D]

continued on next page

5. With the 18-gauge drill bit, drill a hole into the center of the other half of the cups. [E]

6. Sand the edges of each cup until when held together, there are no gaps. The seam must be perfectly flush all the way around. Anneal, pickle, and quench.

7. Place 3 to 4 pieces of hard solder for each pearl on your soldering platform. Flux each cup. Heat the cup until it turns yellow and one by one, transfer each piece of solder to the rim of the cups, placing them approximately ⅛ inch (3 mm) apart. Pickle and quench. [F]

8. Use a damaged Silquar Soldering Board to balance the pearl. Another option is to create a nest with stainless steel binding wire. If you're choosing my method, set the cup with the nip in a cavity in your soldering platform. Balance the cup with the solder and hole on top. Flux. Check to make sure the seam is flush all the way around.

Secure the sphere by holding your pick on the top next to the hole until the flux has foamed.

Heat the entire sphere, focusing a little more on the bottom cup to coax the solder downward. The solder should run all the way around the seam. [G, H]

If there is an air pocket in your first attempt at solder flow, wait until the sphere cools to room temperature. Re-flux. Pick an additional piece of hard solder to the outside of the seam.

Do not pickle or quench. Wait for the pearl to cool to room temperature. Use sandpaper to grind off excess solder and conceal the seam.

9. If you're confident that your seams are securely soldered, close the pinholes. Place 1-inch (2.5 cm) lengths of 18-gauge wire into each pinhole. One at a time, hold the wire steady with the third hand. [I]

Sweat medium solder to the wire. Heat the entire piece until the metal turns yellow. Change the angle of your torch so that you're heating the wire and not the pearl. Continue heating until the solder puddles on the wire. Once it does, turn your torch downward to the pearl to draw the solder from the wire down into the hole.

Repeat this step until each pearl is closed. Leave the excess wire intact. Pickle, quench, and set aside. [J, K, L]

10. With flush cutters, snip the 16-gauge wire into the following lengths:

- 2 @ 2½ inches (6.3 cm)

- 3 @ 1½ inches (3.8 cm)

11. As instructed in the barbell chain tutorial, add lollipop loops to one or both ends of the wires as follows:

- Both ends of the 2 @ 2½ inches (6.3 cm)

- One end of 1 @ 1½ inches (3.8 cm)

Fuse the lollipop loops closed and hammer them flat.

continued on next page

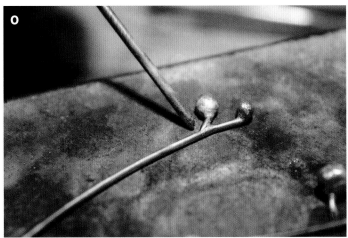

12. Ball the ends of each 3 @ 1½-inch (3.8 cm) wire. You should now have the following:

- 2 @ 2½-inch (6.3 cm) wires with a lollipop loop on each end

- 2 @1½-inch (3.8 cm) wires with one lollipop loop and one ball on either end

- 1 @ 1½-inch (3.8 cm) wire with a ball on one end [M]

13. Before connecting, clean up the pearl seams using the black silicone polishing disc. [N]

14. At this point, you'll begin to connect the pearls to the strands. Begin with the smallest pearls. Snip the excess 18-gauge wire so that it measures approximately ¼ inch (6 mm) and bend it slightly with your fingers.

One by one, figure out where you want to place each pearl. You can do this one at a time as you progress through each solder joint. Snip the 18-gauge wire at an angle so that it sits flush with the 16-gauge strand where you intend to solder it.

15. Flux a small pearl. Sweat hard solder to the end of the stem. Hold the pearl in a third hand or cross locking tweezers so that the stem sits flush against the 16-gauge strand. Flux. Focus the heat primarily on the 16-gauge wire to draw the solder over from the 18-gauge wire. Pickle and quench. [O]

Repeat this step until you have soldered all of the small pearls to their designated strands. [P]

Situate the cross-locking tweezers between the previously soldered pearls and the next one you will solder. The tweezers will act as a heat sink to protect your previous solder joints.

16. Flux a large pearl. Sweat medium solder to the end of the stem. Hold the pearl in a third hand so that the stem sits flush against the 16-gauge strand.

Continue as instructed in step 14.

17. Finally, solder together the 2 @ 1½-inch (3.8 cm) wires with one lollipop loop and one ball on either end to the 2 @ 2½-inch (6.3 cm) wires with a lollipop loop on each end. Use the cross-locking tweezers to protect all previous solder joints.

18. Make a ball rivet: Snip a ¼-inch (6 mm) piece of 18-gauge wire. With your torch, ball one end.

19. Marry the bottom 2½-inch (6.3 cm) to the top 1½-inch (3.8 cm) lollipop loops. Stick the ball rivet through each of the lollipop loops. [Q]

Balance the links together on your soldering platform so that the rivet is pointing upwards, like the bicycle chain. With your torch angled directly at the pin, use a high heat to ball it downward. Pickle and quench. [R]

20. Remove sharp spots with the black silicone polishing disc. Finish as desired. [S]

Think Happy Accidents

IMAGINE: YOU'VE SPENT AN ENTIRE MORNING SAWING, forming, filing, and sanding until all joints are flush, soldering one, two, and three of those joints. As you're soldering your fourth and last joint, you're holding your breath, and you burn a hole in the back of your silver sheet.

> *"We don't make mistakes, just happy little accidents."*
>
> **—BOB ROSS, ARTIST AND HOST OF** *THE JOY OF PAINTING*

I can appreciate the worry that accompanies making mistakes. Precious metal isn't cheap, and it can be devastating to invest so many hours into a piece only to think you have destroyed it. Yes, we can recycle silver into sheet and send our scraps in for cash, but that doesn't account for our time spent making.

No matter how many of us have dressed up as Bob Ross for Halloween, his words do ring true. The majority of the skills I've obtained have stemmed from making mistakes.

So, what if you have burnt a hole through your silver sheet? Instead of scrapping the piece altogether, can you challenge yourself to repair it? Can you turn it into something different than you initially intended?

Perhaps, if you burn a hole in a carefully fabricated leaf, you can add an inchworm to make the hole appear intentional. If you accidentally reticulate the edge of a flower petal, you can add a ladybug in the empty space. If you have your heart and mind set on a leaf or flower without insects, there are ways in which you can mend your work without starting over. All of these techniques will undoubtedly add to your skill set. So, rather than fretting about making mistakes, I encourage you to reframe your mindset to take each step as a new challenge that, in the end, will contribute to you becoming a master silversmith.

When I first began my silversmithing journey, I was extremely conservative with my saw lines, trying to make the most use of each sterling silver sheet I purchased. As I learned how to make chains, melted links were tossed aside with a groan, my pile of scrap inevitably growing. When sawing, I caught silver dust and filtered any other dust out of my vacuum bag. Eventually, I had enough silver to ship in exchange for cash.

At some point, I realized that it was more orderly to return-for-refund smooth rather than sharp, jagged metal, so I began to melt all of my scraps into "buttons." And then I realized I could incorporate the buttons into jewelry designs.

If your brain churns with ideas as much as mine does, you probably understand waking up in the middle of the night with a persistent idea preventing further sleep. It was during one of these restless hours that I contemplated melting catawampus chain links into the shape of a branch. Successfully experimenting with fusing and carving opened up an entirely new dimension to silversmithing and more elaborate projects like dragonflies, butterflies, frogs, beetles, a praying mantis, walking stick, and eventually a hummingbird and life-sized swallow.

Once I realized that I could not only repair my accidents but use the scraps to push boundaries, three important things happened:

1. I stopped sending scrap metal in for a refund.

2. I no longer worried about making mistakes, which also meant that I stopped holding my breath.

3. Relaxed breathing led to me being more relaxed with my torch, which also translated to immensely improved torch control.

When you're disappointed that you have damaged a piece, I encourage you to stop, breathe, and look at your piece through a different lens. Can you add a decorative or playful patch? Can you take your accident one further to make your silver appear even more alive than you intended?

In the projects that follow, we'll explore some of these possibilities. I guarantee that you, too, will be amazed at how far you can stretch the boundaries with silver. With time, you'll worry less, breathe more, and gain increased torch control.

Branches

As I climb peaks, meander through our mountain meadows, walk beaches, and stroll along river-banks, my eyes are endlessly surveying my natural surroundings. I search for heart rocks, intriguing seedpods and lichen-covered bark, withering leaves, dead insects, feathers, and anything with intricate textures or convoluted forms. My brain automatically begins to dissect what I hold in my hand, and I find myself eager to escape to my studio.

When you prune a shrub or tree, take a moment to absorb the texture of its branches. Rub your fingers gently down the branch to feel how smooth or abrasive it is and how the texture changes closer to

the tip. Does the grain interlock like that of a sycamore, or is it narrow, slender, and three-angled like a larch? How far apart are each of the nodes, and does the branch zigzag in between like that of a hawthorn?

I've grown more observant since I first began fabricating branches, so my techniques have broadened tremendously in scope. The following tutorial will walk you through the first style of branch I made, resembling that of an elm. The second, a cottonwood branch, will involve a few extra steps.

ELM BRANCH

Tools and Materials

Smith Little Torch Propane and Oxygen System with #6 torch tip

Silquar Soldering Board

Sterling silver scrap wire (including catawampus chain links)

Flush cutters

Titanium pick

Copper tongs

Flex shaft or high-speed Dremel Rotary Tool

Carbide cone bur

Separating disc

Small cross cut cylinder bur

Small round bur (optional)

Black silicone polishing disc

Liver of sulfur, dry concentrate (optional)

Coarse fiber wheel

Mild dish soap and water

Techniques

Fusing wire

Manipulating silver with the heat of the torch

Carving with the flex shaft

The benefit of heat sinks

1. Arrange several pieces of wire in the general shape of the branch you intend to make. The gauge of the wire doesn't matter, and the gauges can be different. Just be sure that it's all sterling silver. Do not add fine silver when fusing sterling because the fine silver will initially float around within the sterling. When it does eventually melt, it will rise to and remain on the surface and prevent you from being able to roll your fused form (step 9 below). [A]

2. With flush cutters, snip little pieces of sterling silver wire or sheet and set them on the side of your soldering platform.

3. When fusing, no solder is necessary. Therefore, you do not need flux.

continued on next page

4. To begin fusing, focus your torch on the center of the mass, the center of the pile of wires. Use your pick to nudge the wires together to ensure that they are touching. If they aren't, the wire will ball up rather than fuse. Once the wires begin to fuse, move your flame from one end to the other. The wire should pull together and fuse as you're moving from the center of the mass to each end. [B, C]

5. *Optional step.* Fuse together a second, smaller pile of wires to create a side branch from an axillary bud, repeating the instructions in step 4.

6. If you have opted for step 5, fuse the two components of the branch together, focusing your torch on the mass so that the offshoot, the smaller and therefore more heat-vulnerable piece, doesn't ball up. Use your pick to nudge the two together. Once the heat mass is sufficiently hot and molten, move your torch to the spot where they're connecting to finish the fuse. You might notice that this technique is similar to making the links for the barbell chain. [D]

7. At this point, you can manipulate the metal with the heat of your torch. If there's one section of your branch that needs more mass and another that contains an unwanted blob, you can draw the silver back and forth. To do so, heat the "blob" until it becomes molten. As soon as it does, use the heat of your torch to coax it toward a spot that contains less mass. The molten silver will follow the heat of your torch. It will stop moving once it's no longer molten. Repeat this step until you're happy with the distribution of the mass. The goal is to hard-fuse the branch. [E, F]

8. To prevent your silver from splaying outward, change the angle of your torch so that you're heating the sides of the branch, not only the top. If you overheat the silver or focus solely on the top, it will puddle and adhere to the soldering platform. In this case, wait for both the silver and soldering platform to cool. Gently pull the silver off the soldering platform and ensure that it's clean. If not, either file or grind off all debris. Turn the silver upside down and heat it from the other side.

9. Once you're happy with the branch dimensions, turn it over to round out the back side which is flat. Do not bring the entire piece to a melting point. Instead, heat the surface of the mass by running your torch slowly and methodically back and forth along the top and sides. Pay attention to ensure that your torch is angled to heat across the top of the branch rather than down and directly into the mass.

continued on next spread

Scan to watch
a video tutorial

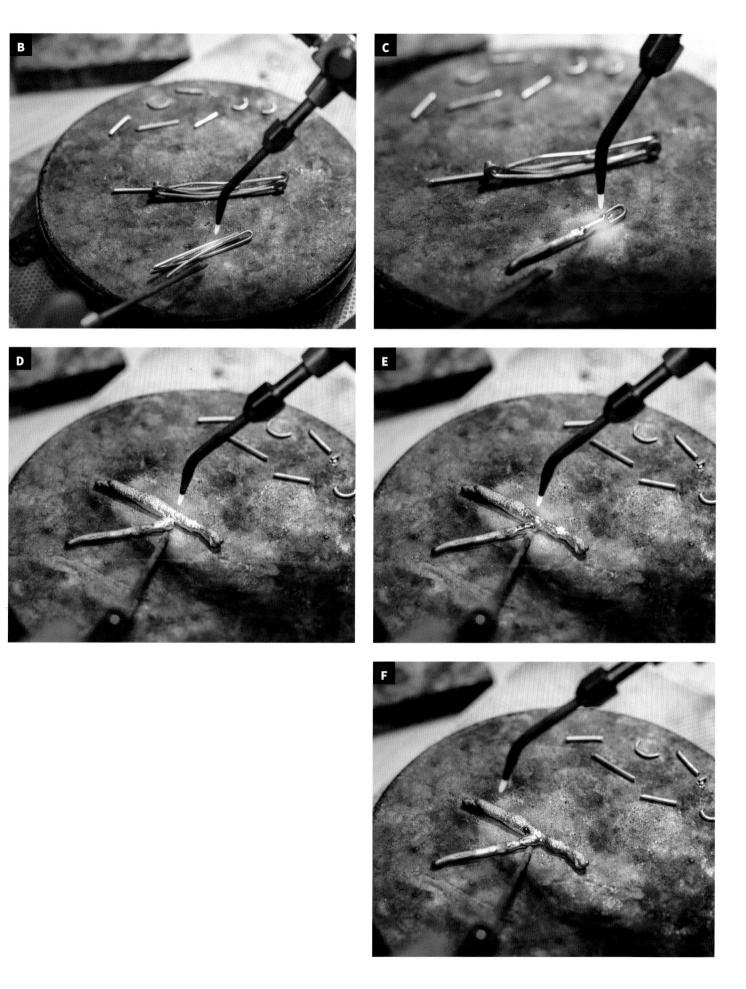

10. To add the nodes, melt each tiny scrap of silver previously set aside. Heat the silver, not your pick, to pick up and transfer the scraps. If your pick gets too hot and won't pick up the silver, stick it in your quench and try again. Heat the branch, the mass. Focus your flame on the branch BELOW where you intend to place the node so that it appears as if it's growing upward. You can use your pick as a heat sink in the upper inside of the node to prevent it from fusing to the branch. That way, your node will look like it's growing upward rather than an undefined lump. [G, H, I]

11. Don't worry too much about how your branch looks at this point. You'll be surprised at how much it will improve when you've worked on it with the flex shaft.

12. *Optional step.* Add previously fused jump rings to each end so you can incorporate the branch into a chain or pendant. To do so, place the jump ring up against the branch. Focus your torch on the mass (the branch), not the jump ring. If you focus on the jump ring, it'll melt. Watch the metal as you're heating. Once it's red and molten, move the flame toward the jump ring until they fuse. You can place the tip of your pick inside the jump ring as a heat sink to protect it from melting. [J]

13. Use the carbide cone bur to shave off unwanted blemishes. Sweep the shards to the side so that you do not get slivers stuck in your skin. Save the shards for future projects. Instructions for fusing dust will be included in the next branch tutorial. Continue to shave until you're happy with the shape of the branch. This will also remove potential fire scale caused by the intense heat of your torch. [K]

14. Use the separating disc to fine-tune hard to reach spots and to accentuate the nodes. [L]

15. Use a smaller cross cut cylinder bur to scribble texture into the branch. You may also opt to use a round bur to add subtle texture around the nodes. [M]

16. Smooth down the silver using the black silicone polishing disc, rounding out sharp or pointed spots. [N]

17. *Optional step.* Patina your branch using liver of sulfur (see "Steps for Finishing Your Work," page 150).

18. Remove some of the patina with a coarse fiber wheel.

19. Rinse and wash your branch with mild soap and water.

Fire Stain and Fire Scale

I'm often asked about fire stain and fire scale that happens when applying high heat to sterling silver, particularly without the use of flux.

Fire stain is a layer of oxides that is visible on the surface of the silver. On copper-containing alloys of gold or of silver (such as sterling silver), it appears as a red or purple stain, disrupting the bright polished surface of the finished piece. It's sometimes referred to incorrectly as fire *scale*.

Fire scale is a flaky deposit that can occur on the surface of nonferrous metals when heated.

Given that the fire stain layer is usually not very deep, it can often be removed by polishing, sanding, grinding, filing, and wire brushing. Traditional silversmiths may worry about the loss of material or fine details to the piece. With my approach, however, it's not a concern since I do frequently shave off the surface layer and carve details into the mass.

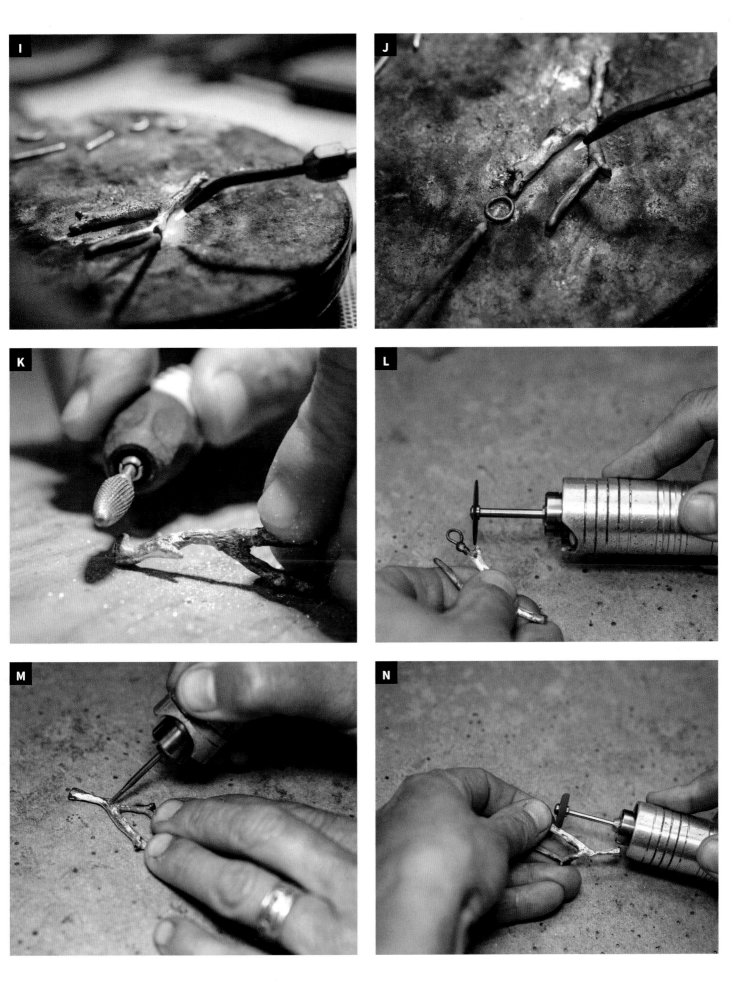

COTTONWOOD BRANCH

Tools and Materials

Smith Little Torch Propane and Oxygen System with #6 and #7 torch tips

Silquar Soldering Board

One to two 3" (7.5 cm) lengths of sterling silver scrap edges

1" (2.5 cm) 21-gauge sterling silver wire

Cross locking tweezers

Carbide cone bur

Flex shaft or high-speed Dremel Rotary Tool

Black silicone polishing disc

Silver dust

Third hand tool

Titanium pick

Copper tongs

Liver of sulfur, dry concentrate (optional)

Coarse fiber wheel

Mild dish soap and water

Techniques

Fusing sterling silver scraps

Manipulating silver with the heat of the torch

Carving with the flex shaft

The benefit of heat sinks

Fusing sterling silver dust

1. For this particular branch, begin by "slumping" the edges of the scrap sterling silver. To do so, hold the silver in cross locking tweezers. With the #6 torch tip, angle your torch across the top of the silver until it begins to melt. Slowly move your torch across the top as the metal slumps. When you've made your way across one side, turn the scrap over to repeat this step on the opposite side. Depending on the initial dimensions of the scrap, you may be able to do this a few times.

2. Set the silver scrap on the soldering platform. Continue to direct the heat on the sides of the scrap so that it draws inward. As soon as it draws into a substantial mass with a rounded top, begin to log roll and redistribute the mass as needed. Quench when finished. [A]

3. Tightly wrap the 21-gauge wire around the mass in all sorts of random directions. Overlap the wire, leaving some areas thin and others thick. [B]

4. You may need to switch to a #7 torch tip if the mass is quite large. I suggest starting with a #6 torch tip and switching to a #7 if necessary.

Hold your torch tip close and heat in between the wrapped wire, directing your torch at the mass within. As soon as the mass turns red and begins to "soft-fuse" to the wire, move your torch back.

It's okay if pieces of wire split apart and ball up. That will add to the knobby nature of the branch.

Log roll and continue to soft-fuse the wire to the mass until there are no remaining gaps. [C, D]

continued on next page

5. Hold the branch vertically in cross locking tweezers with one side resting on the soldering platform.

Point your torch tip directly at the base of the branch. Allow the weight of the branch to do the work. Additional pressure might snap the piece apart. After a few moments, the branch will slump, creating a solid pith. [E, F]

6. If you intend to add fused jump rings, do so at this time.

7. Use the carbide cone bur to shave off unwanted blemishes and to accentuate curves. Save the silver dust. [G]

8. Smooth down the silver using the black silicone polishing disc, rounding out sharp or pointed spots. Rinse. [H]

9. Place the branch in water. While it's wet, sprinkle a thick layer of silver dust across one side of the branch. [I]

10. Place the branch in the third hand. Heat the branch from below and watch as the silver dust turns from white to yellow, gold, and black. [J, K]

As soon as the silver dust turns black, support the underside of the branch with your pick and heat the branch from above.

Slowly move your torch in concentrated circular motions across the branch as the metal turns red and the silver dust stops glowing. Quench and repeat this step on the other side.

11. You may need to repeat step 10 as needed.

12. *Optional step.* Patina your branch using liver of sulfur.

13. Remove some of the patina with a coarse fiber wheel.

14. Rinse and wash your branch with mild soap and water. [L]

Salmon

MY INTEREST IN STUDYING AND FABRICATING endangered plant and animal species sparked as I continued my silversmithing journey. In addition, with my growing audience on social media, I felt a responsibility to join the movement to educate others about the impacts of plant and animal extinction on the rest of the ecosystem.

Salmon are a common place to begin given their enormous impact on our environment. At least 137 different species depend on the marine-rich nutrients that wild salmon provide. Their perilous, exhausting annual journey, sometimes hundreds of miles long against the current, is a miracle of nature.

Some species of salmon are considered *keystone species*, which means that they are vital to sustaining their ecosystems. The sockeye salmon, for example, is a keystone species in Alaska's Bristol Bay, situated in Katmai National Park. After the salmon spawn and ultimately perish, their decomposing carcasses fertilize the soil of the riverbanks and boreal forests. The plants absorb the nutrients, which then nourishes the animals that live and thrive in the region. Unfortunately, sockeye salmon are vulnerable to many stressors and threats including blocked access to spawning grounds and habitat degradation caused by dams and culverts.

The Atlantic salmon, listed as an endangered species in the United States and susceptible to the same hazards, is considered an *indicator species*, which means that its own health reflects the health of its ecosystem. When a river ecosystem is clean and well connected, its salmon population is typically healthy and robust. However, when a river ecosystem becomes polluted or disrupted, there will be a noticeable decrease in its salmon population.

Since each part of a salmon's life cycle is so heavily interconnected with its surrounding environment, if the salmon population continues to decline, such as that of the Pacific sockeye salmon, then the entire ecosystem will fail.

Here are just a few things we can do to help:

Wash your cars on your lawn or at a car wash to prevent harmful chemicals from flowing down the storm drain.

Conserve water.

Choose all-natural cleaning products or try making your own to reduce the amount of chemicals you pour down the drain.

Limit using pesticides, weed killers, and fertilizers.

Landscape with native, drought-resistant plants.

Choose products without packaging, such as bulk items and loose produce, and bring your own bags.

See how you can get involved in salmon recovery efforts in your community.

Tools and Materials

Smith Little Torch Propane and Oxygen System with #7 torch tip

Silquar Soldering Board

Sterling silver scraps

One 3 inch x 3 inch (7.6 x 7.6 cm) 22-gauge sterling silver sheet (You'll only need small pieces of this, so I tend to scrounge through my pile of scraps.)

Titanium pick

Copper tongs

Cross locking tweezers

Flex shaft or high-speed Dremel Rotary Tool

Carbide cone bur

Pencil or Sharpie Permanent Marker, Ultra Fine Point

GreenLion Saw Frame

2/0 and 3/0 saw blades

Bench pin

Bench vise or ring clamp (optional)

Round burs

Small cross cut cylinder bur

Separating disc

Tracing paper

Rubber cement

Diamond knife edge bur

Hard, medium, and easy solder

Two third hand tools

Black silicone polishing disc

Liver of sulfur, dry concentrate (optional)

Coarse fiber wheel

Extra easy solder (optional)

Mild dish soap and water

Techniques

Fusing sterling silver scraps

Manipulating silver with the heat of the torch

Carving with the flex shaft

Sawing

Texturing with the flex shaft

Soldering multiple joints to a fused mass

The benefit of heat sinks

1. Start by melting sterling silver scraps into a collection of "buttons" of varying sizes. Remember that when fusing, no solder is necessary, and be sure not to include any fine silver scraps. Set the buttons aside and let them cool to room temperature.

2. Arrange the buttons in the general shape of the salmon body that you envision. The gauge of the wire doesn't matter, and the gauges can be different. [A]

3. To begin fusing the buttons together, focus your torch on the bottom center of the mass. [B]

   Once the buttons begin to fuse together, slowly move your flame outward toward both its head and tail. As soon as all of the buttons have soft-fused, turn the entire mass over to heat the opposite side. This will prevent the piece from adhering to the soldering platform, and you can begin to log roll. [C, D]

4. Continuously change the angle of your torch to heat the sides and top of the mass until all of the buttons are "hard-fused."

   If you overheat the silver or focus solely on the top, it'll pool outwards and stick to the soldering platform. If this happens, as stated in chapter 8, wait for both the silver and soldering platform to cool. Gently remove the silver from the soldering platform and ensure that it's clean of any debris.

   You may need to add more buttons on the flat side of the salmon to give it more dimension. [E, F]

5. You can use your pick to slump the body, which will make your salmon appear as though it's swimming. To do so, place your pick below the body while heating the top. Continue to heat until the silver slumps. The silver may crack, in which case, keep your pick beneath the mass while simultaneously moving the metal with your torch to fill in the crack. [G, H]

continued on next spread

6. Similar to the process in making a branch, if there's one section of your salmon that needs more mass and another that contains an extra "adhesion," heat the "adhesion" until it becomes molten. Use the heat of your torch to coax the molten silver toward a spot that contains less mass. The molten silver will follow the heat of your torch. It will stop in place once it has cooled. Repeat this step until you're content with the distribution of the mass. You may also need to add another small button or two to fill in air pockets. Another option is to hold sterling silver wire in cross locking tweezers and fuse the wire into the air pockets.

7. Continue to log roll the mass. Heat the surface of the mass by running your torch slowly and methodically back and forth along the top and sides. This will help smooth out the surface of the silver to minimize the amount you will later need to shave off. You'll be amazed at how much the body will resemble a salmon once you do some work with the flex shaft. [I]

8. Use the carbide cone bur to shave off unwanted blemishes. Sweep the shards to the side so that you do not get slivers stuck in your skin. Save the shards for future projects. Continue to shave until you've achieved the shape of the salmon. [J, K]

9. With a pencil or Sharpie, draw the shape of the salmon's mouth on its body. The mouth may or may not contain teeth depending on what it eats. If it does have teeth, don't worry about that until step 11.

10. Use a size 2/0 saw blade to saw out the shape of the mouth. You may want to clamp the salmon using a vise or ring clamp to keep it sturdy while sawing. [L]

11. Carve out the inside of the mouth with a round bur. The width of the mouth will determine the size of the round bur you'll use.

    Note. The sharper the bur, the easier it'll be for you to carve out the inside of the mouth. Again, save the silver shavings for future use. Then, if the salmon has teeth, you can cut them into the sides of the mouth with a diamond knife edge bur.

12. Next, with the edge of a cross cut cylinder bur, carve out the operculum (covering the gills) and gill line, and you can accentuate the sides of the mouth. Use the separating disc to deepen the lines. [M, N]

continued on next spread

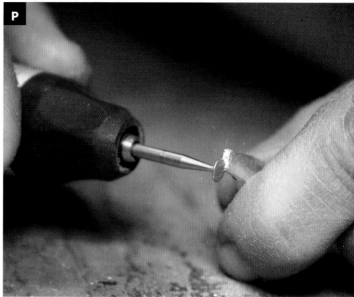

13. Mark exactly where you would like the eyes to go. Use a round bur to carve out a cavity on either side of its head. Then, set the salmon body aside. [O]

14. In my continuous effort to maintain a small footprint on Earth, instead of tracing paper, I like to use the recycled tissue paper that comes wrapped around silver sheet from the wholesale supplier. Whichever you choose, you can draw or trace the fins onto the paper and glue the paper to your sterling silver sheet. Saw out the shapes. Rub off the paper and glue.

15. For each fin, measure and mark a line from one side to the other on the salmon body where you want them to be soldered. Then, use the diamond knife edge bur to precisely carve slots into the body. Carve troughs that are wide enough for the 22-gauge sheet and deep enough for 1 mm of the edge to fit inside. [P, Q, R]

16. Pickle the salmon body to ensure that it's clean and white. It's important for you to watch the colors as you're soldering the fins.

17. Melt 2 tiny pieces of scrap into buttons. They need to be small enough to fit into the eye sockets. Flux and sweat hard solder onto the buttons. [S]

18. Sweat hard solder to the back side of the pectoral fins. Pickle and quench.

19. Remove the salmon from the pickle. Quench. One side at a time, place the eye into the socket and one of the pectoral fins to the side of the body near the operculum. Flux the entire mass. Heat the mass. Ensure that you're focusing your heat on the entire mass, not just where you want the solder to flow. Watch closely as the color of the silver turns from white to yellow. As soon as the yellow begins to dull, you have reached the solder flow point. When the solder flows, pickle the salmon, quench, and repeat these steps on the other side. [T]

continued on next spread

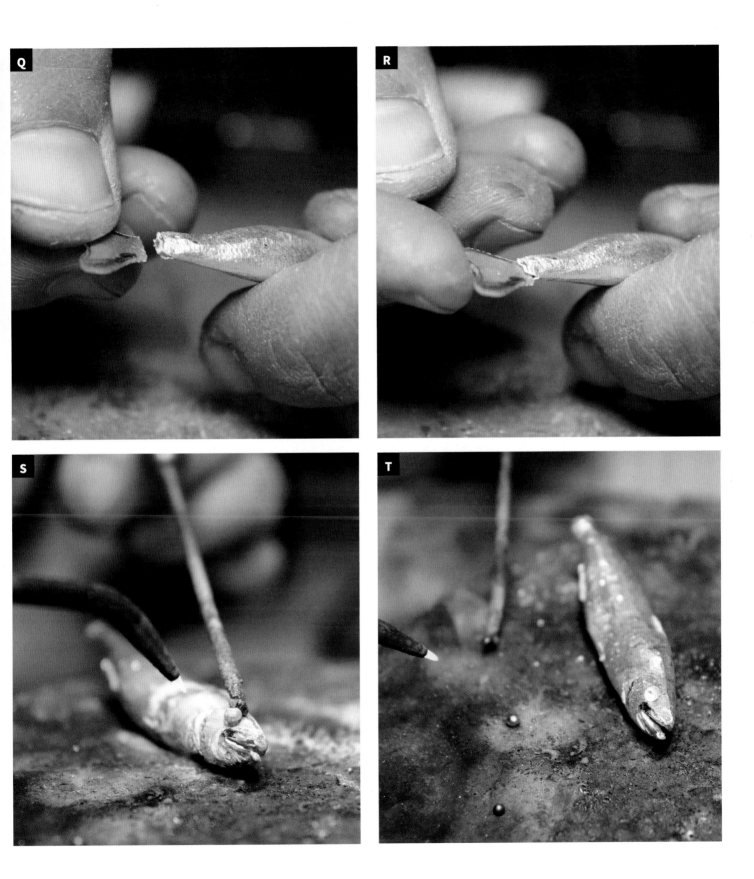

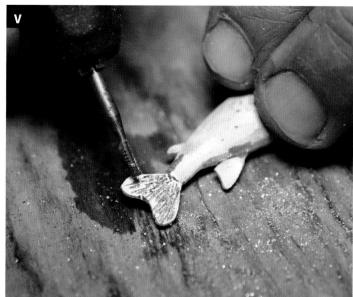

20. The next several solder jobs will require heat sinks. I favor using the GRS Third-Hand with Base since it provides a sturdiness I haven't found in any other third hand.

To protect the eyes and pectoral fins from coming loose, place the salmon body in a third hand, being sure to cross the jaws either over the previous solder joints or between the previous solder joints and the portion of the mass you plan to heat. The salmon should be situated with its back facing up. Set the dorsal fin and adipose fin (small fin located behind the dorsal fin) in their designated troughs. Flux the entire mass.

Set aside several pieces of medium solder and make sure that your pick is clean. If it's coated with solder or residue, grind, or file it off.

21. Heat the mass, focusing your heat on the middle and bottom of the salmon. Avoid directly heating the third hand and front of the salmon. With this method, it'll get hot, but not enough for the previous solder joints to flow. Again, watch as the color of the silver turns from white to yellow.

22. As soon as the silver is yellow, turn your torch downward to the solder. Heat the solder (not your pick) to pick it up. Return your attention to the salmon that is still HOT. As you heat the front side of the joint between the body and the dorsal fin, place the solder on the back side of the joint. Solder follows heat, so your solder should glom onto the spot where it is placed.

Note. You do not need the solder to flow at this point. Repeat this step with the adipose fin. [U]

Now, it's time to coax your solder into and along the seams of the fins. To do so, continue heating the front of the salmon, focusing between the front center of the body and the front center of the fins. If your solder is situated on the left side of the fins, focus your heat to the right to coax the solder directly into and along the seam of the fin.

Once the solder has successfully flowed, pickle and quench the salmon. Be careful, the third hand might be hot to the touch. I keep miniature oven mitts on my bench for this purpose.

23. Turn the salmon upside down. The salmon should be situated with its belly facing up. Place cross locking tweezers over both the dorsal and adipose fins. Cross the third hand jaws over the hard solder joints. Situate the pelvic and anal fins in their designated troughs. Flux the entire mass.

Again, set aside several pieces of medium solder. (*Optional:* You can use easy solder instead if you prefer.)

Repeat the soldering instructions outlined in step 21.

24. Turn the salmon so that its mouth is resting on your soldering platform. Secure the hard solder joints with the cross locking tweezers. Twist a third hand so that it clamps across both the dorsal and adipose fins. Clamp a second third hand across the pelvic and anal fins. Set the caudal fin (tail fin) in its trough.

Set aside two pieces of easy solder. (*Optional:* You may use extra easy solder if you prefer.)

Repeat the soldering instructions outlined in step 21, but this time focusing your heat straight down the lateral line of the body. Again, if your solder is situated on the left side of the caudal fin, focus your heat to the right to coax the solder directly into and along the seam.

Pickle and quench.

25. With the small cross cut cylinder bur, carve lines into both sides of each of the fins to resemble spines. Anneal, pickle, and quench. [V]

26. *Optional step.* With a round bur, add texture on both sides of the salmon body to resemble its speckled coloring. [W]

27. Smooth down the silver using the black silicone polishing disc, rounding out sharp or pointed spots.

28. *Optional step.* Patina your salmon using liver of sulfur. Remove some of the patina with a coarse fiber wheel.

29. Rinse and wash your finished piece with mild soap and water. [X]

Ode to a Dragonfly

I ALMOST ALWAYS DRAW MY OWN INSPIRATION FROM MY IMMEDIATE SURROUNDINGS. Back in August 2017, as my husband and I sat on our patio watching the sunset and relishing the cooler evening temperature, we witnessed thousands of dragonflies swarm above our home. We watched them with awe and wonder. I later read that they may have been feeding or swarming before migration.

Dragonflies are important to their environments both as predators (particularly of mosquitos) and as prey to birds and fish. Because they require stable oxygen levels and clean water, scientists consider them reliable bioindicators of healthy freshwater ecosystems.

Over 16 percent of the world's dragonfly and damselfly species are under threat of extinction. Their decline is the result of the widespread loss of the marshes, swamps, and free-flowing rivers they breed in, mostly driven by the expansion of unsustainable agriculture and urbanization.

Here are just a few ways that we can help:

Use rain barrels to help reduce the impact of stormwater on local streams.

Install a backyard dragonfly pool to attract dragonflies, damselflies, frogs, salamanders, butterflies, songbirds, box turtles, and native bees to your landscape.

Do not release exotic/non-native animals into your watershed.

Minimize your use of fertilizers and pesticides.

Plant a native buffer along the shoreline of every stream.

It just so happened that, the morning following the swarm, I arrived at my studio to find a dead dragonfly on my concrete floor. Naturally, I picked it up, turned it over in my hands to study the shape of its body, thorax, abdominal segments, its face and eyes, and the texture of its wings. I instantly knew that my plans for the day were thwarted and that, instead of making what I anticipated, I would try my hand at fabricating a dragonfly.

Tools and Materials

Smith Little Torch Propane and Oxygen System with #6 torch tip

Silquar Soldering Board

22-gauge sterling silver sheet

4" (10 cm) 21-gauge wire

Sterling silver scraps

Tracing paper (optional)

Rubber cement

GreenLion Saw Frame

2/0 saw blade

Bench pin

Titanium pick

Copper tongs

Two third hand tools

Carbide cone bur

Flex shaft or high-speed Dremel

Rotary Tool

Separating disc

Black silicone polishing disc

Easy, medium, and hard solder

2mm cross cut cylinder bur

Pencil or Sharpie Permanent Marker, Ultra Fine Point

Drill bit for 21-gauge wire

Flush cutters

My-T-Flux or similar liquid hard-soldering flux

Bales (optional)

Liver of sulfur, dry concentrate (optional)

Coarse fiber wheel (optional)

Mild dish soap and water

Techniques

Sawing

Fusing

Carving fused form

Sweat soldering

Soldering wire perpendicular to sheet

Soldering to fused form

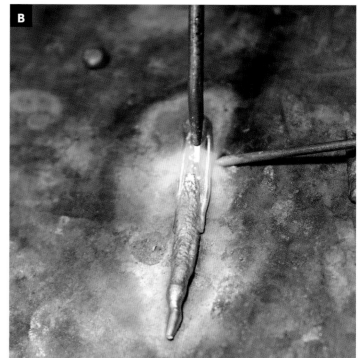

1. To obtain the shape of the dragonfly wings, you can print an image directly from your computer or trace an image from your phone. Glue and paste the image to 22-gauge silver sheet.

2. Saw around the outline of the wings. Rub off the paper and glue. Anneal, pickle, and quench the wings. Set them aside.

3. The first step in forging the form is to fuse the thorax and abdomen.

   Using the same techniques outlined in the Branch tutorial, begin by fusing the scrap wire for the abdomen.

   Arrange the melted scraps in the general shape of the dragonfly body. Begin heating the center of the mass. When your silver buttons and abdomen fuse together, move your torch outward to the edges. Log roll the body as you heat so that it doesn't adhere to the soldering platform. Play around with the idea of "painting" with your torch. Get used to moving it back and forth. [A, B]

   Note. Use the tip of your pick as a heat sink if you're worried about the abdomen shrinking. If you do lose some length in the abdomen, you'll need to add more wire to the end in order to draw additional mass outward. [C]

   Continue to log roll the dragonfly to redistribute mass as needed and to round out each side. Add more material if needed and use the heat of your torch to redistribute mass. [D, E]

4. Now, you'll fuse the head to the thorax. Place the dragonfly in a pair of third hands, abdomen-down and resting on the soldering platform.

   With high heat, turn your torch downward into the mass. Your goal is to slump the top of the thorax so that there is a flat spot for the head to rest upon. Another option would be to saw or file a flat spot, but this is an excellent exercise that will further your understanding of how to manipulate molten metal. [F, G]

   Place another small button on top of the flattened thorax.

   Now, turn your torch to heat directly between the top of the thorax and the head until the two have soft-fused. Rotate your torch around the seam until the entire seam has soft-fused. Pickle and quench. [H]

5. Use the carbide cone bur to shave off any unwanted blemishes from the dragonfly body. I often leave the thorax untouched during this process to mimic its naturally mottled appearance. [I]

continued on next spread

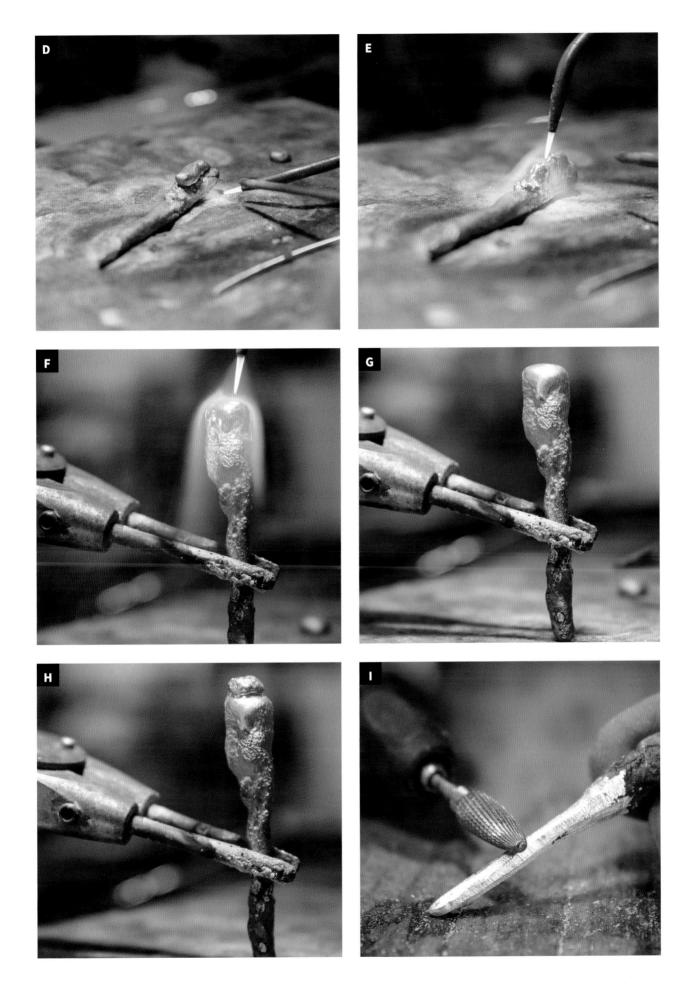

6. Use the separating disc to bring definition to the head and body and to create the abdominal segments. [J]

To carve out the abdominal segments, start with the segment that is closest to the thorax. Carve a shallow groove all the way around the abdomen.

Continue carving segments, one at a time, until you reach the cerci (the terminal appendages), which you'll also fine-tune with the separating disc. [K, L]

7. Sand down any jagged spots with the black silicone polishing disc. Anneal, pickle, quench, and set the body aside. [M]

8. Take your pre-annealed wings and lay them flat on your soldering platform. Lay a piece of 21-gauge wire across the top of each wing.

Scan to watch a video tutorial

Note. Be sure to leave ⅛ inch (3 mm) hanging off the inside edge of each wing. [N]

Place 2 small pieces of easy solder next to the wire on each wing.

With the heat of your torch, draw the solder up onto the wire and wait until it puddles. [O]

Focus the heat of your torch on the sheet (the mass) to coax the solder from the wire down below. Pickle and quench. [P]

Optional step. You can add more dimension to the wings by adding 2 to 3 additional pieces of wire to each wing. Repeat step 9 above. [Q, R]

continued on next spread

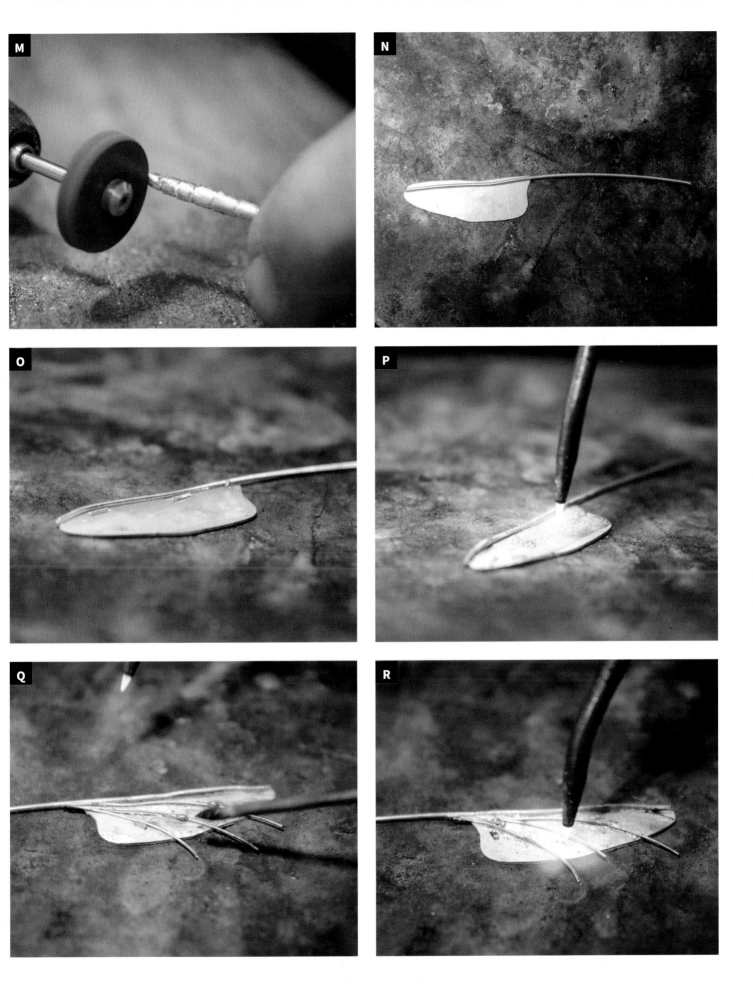

9. Use the separating disc and black silicone polishing disc to blend the wire into the wings and file down the edges. [S]

10. With the small cross cut cylinder bur, in between the 21-gauge wire, scribble across the surface of the wings in all different directions. [T]

11. Situate the wings next to the body. With a pencil or Sharpie, mark exactly where on top of the thorax you want the four wings to be soldered. [U, V]

Scan to watch
a video tutorial

12. It's such a bummer when a drill bit breaks off into the solid piece of silver. To avoid that, make sure to lubricate the drill bit. Should a bit break off inside the fused mass, it can be removed by soaking the piece in a strong pickle.

Carefully drill 4 holes. [W]

13. On each wing, bend the excess wire into a 90-degree angle and with flush cutters, snip it so that it fits snugly into its designated hole. [X]

14. Place the wires into the drilled holes and flux. It might seem obvious, but double-check that you've placed the fore and hind wings in their correct positions. I've made the mistake before of switching them around, not realizing my error until they are all securely soldered in. [Y]

Lay hard solder right above the joints. Your goal is to heat the mass below all four joints to coax the solder downward into the holes. [Z]

continued on next page

15. If this seems like too much soldering at one time, try first hard soldering the fore wings and then medium soldering the hind wings. You can use your pick as a heat sink to protect the wings and wires when focusing your torch on the mass. [AA, BB, CC]

16. *Optional step.* Soldering bales across the back of the wings helps increase stability. [DD, EE]

17. Smooth down the silver using the black silicone polishing disc, rounding out sharp or pointed spots.

18. *Optional step.* Patina your dragonfly using liver of sulfur. Remove some of the patina with a coarse fiber wheel.

19. Rinse and wash your finished piece with mild soap and water. [FF]

CC

DD

EE

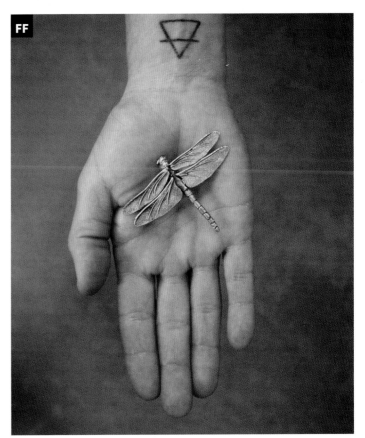

FF

A Migrating Monarch Butterfly

Adult migratory monarch butterflies can be immediately identified by their brilliant orange, black-veined wings adorned with white spots towards the edges. The tiny, delicate creature travels nearly 3,000 miles (4,828 km) from southern Canada and the northern United Sates to its over-wintering destination in Mexico. After mating, they fly another 1,000 miles (1,609 km) to lay their eggs exclusively on milkweed plants, which eventually serves as a food source for the caterpillars. This is one of the world's longest insect migrations.

Unfortunately, the migratory monarch butterfly has decreased by more than 80 percent in the last three decades. Both climate change and the use of herbicides in the United States contribute to the significant loss in milkweed, which is essential for monarchs' reproduction.

Here are just a few ways that we can help:

Plant milkweed.

Plant a wide variety of native flowers that both bloom throughout the monarch's stay and help to promote a diverse and healthy ecosystem.

Find a reputable source for native plants and ask your local garden center to stock native flowers.

Avoid using pesticides.

Spread the word.

Volunteer for habitat restoration projects.

Protect remaining open spaces.

Tools and Materials

Smith Little Torch Propane and Oxygen System with #6 torch tip

Silquar Soldering Board

22-gauge sterling silver sheet

22-gauge brass sheet (optional)

Sterling silver scraps

2" (5 cm) 20-gauge sterling silver wire

Rubber cement

GreenLion Saw Frame

2/0 saw blade

Bench pin

Drill bit for 21-gauge wire

Drill bit for 16-gauge wire

My-T-Flux or similar liquid hard-soldering flux

Easy, medium, and hard solder

2 third hand tools

Titanium pick

Copper tongs

Rawhide mallet (optional)

2mm cross cut cylinder bur (optional)

Carbide cone bur

Flex shaft or high-speed Dremel Rotary Tool

Separating disc

Black silicone polishing disc

Needle-nose pliers

Extra easy solder (optional)

Liver of sulfur, dry concentrate (optional)

Coarse fiber wheel (optional)

Mild dish soap and water

Swanstrom SawPlate System with Gary's Clamp (optional)

Techniques

Piercing and sawing

Sweat soldering

Soldering multiple layers of sheet together

Pick soldering

Fusing

Carving a fused form with flex shaft

Soldering wire perpendicular to sheet

Swanstrom SawPlate System with Gary's Clamp

The Swanstrom SawPlate System with Gary's Clamp helps hold and precisely position your work while piercing and sawing. The aluminum SawPlate can either rotate or lock in place to secure your work. The SawPlate mounts to your bench using the GRS BenchMate System. It comes with three SawPlate clamps, each with an open center and holes that provide flexibility in configuring and holding your pieces. Since the clamps help reduce stress on your hands and fingers when working with small items, I recommend this tool for those who experience difficulty with dexterity.

1. Finding a wing template depicting an entire butterfly with both fore and hind wings outstretched would be ideal. Print two copies and paste the templates to the 22-gauge silver sheet. In other words, you should have eight wings, but leave each pair of fore and hind wing as one piece. Optional: You might opt to use the brass sheet as the underlayer.

2. Saw around the outline of the wing templates. It should appear as though you have two butterfly blanks. Set one aside. If opting to use brass for the underlayer, set that one aside. Rub off the paper and glue.

3. Use the 21-gauge drill bit to pierce each wing cell. Be sure to lubricate the bit periodically as you drill.

4. Thread your blade through each hole and carefully saw around the inside edge of each wing cell. Leave sufficient space so that you do not saw through the wing veins. Anneal, pickle, and quench. [A, B, C]

5. Lay the pre-annealed patterned wings with the back side facing up on your soldering platform. Flux.

Set approximately 20–30 pieces of easy solder all along the wing veins. Gently heat with your torch until the solder has puddled. Pickle and quench. [D, E]

6. Take the mirror image of the wings and place them together, ensuring that the sweat solder is situated between the two layers.

Secure the wings in a pair of third hands. Flux both the top and bottom. Heat evenly across the entire match, primarily from below, until you see the solder flow. Should the silver warp as you heat, use your pick to support the weight. [F, G]

If your solder doesn't flow evenly across the sheet or if the two sheets separate, STOP. Pickle, quench, and hammer them together with a rawhide mallet. Return them to the third hand and repeat the same steps until the solder has flowed evening between the 2 sheets. Pickle and quench.

continued on next spread

7. *Optional step.* Use a small cross cut cylinder bur to add texture to the wings. [H]

8. Lay out the melted scraps in the general shape of the body. Begin heating the center of the mass. When your silver buttons and abdomen fuse together, move your torch outward to the edges. Log roll the body as you heat so that it doesn't adhere to the soldering platform.

   Continue to log roll the butterfly to redistribute mass as needed and to round out each side.

   Log roll the butterfly to round out the bottom side. Pickle and quench. [I]

9. Use the carbide cone bur to shave off any unwanted blemishes from the butterfly body.

10. Use the separating disc to bring more definition to the body and to create the abdominal segments as described in the dragonfly tutorial (step 6).

11. Use the black silicone polishing disc to smooth out any sharp or jagged spots.

12. With the drill bit for the 16-gauge wire, drill a hole in the top of the butterfly's head. [J]

13. Place the body on top of the wings and trace its shape to ensure that when you saw them apart, the lines are flush with the body. [K]

    Saw along the lines.

Then, saw between the fore and hind wings ALMOST but not all the way through. This will create a visual divide.

14. Place the butterfly body on the soldering platform on its side. Use third hands to situate the wings flush against the body. Flux. [L]

    Sweat hard solder immediately against the joints. Your goal is to heat the mass to coax the solder along the seams. Pickle and quench. [M, N]

15. Make the antennae.

    Note. If you plan on including a proboscis (long tongue), you should solder it at the same time as the antennae.

16. Fold the 2 inches (5 cm) of 20-gauge wire in half. Use needle-nose pliers to pinch together the fold. [O]

    Stick the pinched fold into the hole on the top of the butterfly's head. It should be a snug fit.

    With your fingers, bend the wire so that it touches the tops of each wing. Pinch the bend with pliers.

continued on next spread

17. Flux. Sweat solder easy solder to the wire just outside the fold. Once it puddles, focus the heat of your torch on the body of the butterfly until you coax the solder into the hole. [P]

18. Place the butterfly on the soldering platform. Flux. Sweat easy solder to the tips of each antennae that are touching the wings. Then, turn the flame to the wings, heating only the wings (not the wire) until you coax the solder onto the wings. Pickle and quench. [Q]

19. Smooth down the silver using the black silicone polishing disc, rounding out sharp or pointed spots.

20. *Optional step.* Patina your butterfly using liver of sulfur. Remove some of the patina with a coarse fiber wheel.

21. Rinse and wash your finished piece with mild soap and water.

Scan to watch
a video tutorial

Aged Aspen Bark and Lichen

I spent my adolescence in Switzerland and France where my family took advantage of the wide-open mountainous terrain to hike and ski. Switzerland boasts some 65,000 kilometers (40,389 miles) of the longest, densest, most varied, and best marked network of hiking trails. From the snow-capped mountains and glaciers of the Swiss Alps to verdant valleys full of cascading waterfalls and idyllic green pastures with mountain huts where soft-eyed cattle graze, my love of nature was born.

The international school I attended organized weekly field trips for all students to go skiing or orienteering, depending on the time of year. Orienteering is the sport of navigation, using a topographical map and compass to navigate from point to point in diverse and unfamiliar terrain. It was during these timed events that I discovered the beauty of the under forest as I navigated downed logs, boulders, and near-impenetrable thickets, my shoes soggy from running through decomposing plant material.

Did you know that the aspen has a unique lichen flora and that many of the lichens found on aspen are host-specific? That means that they *only* live on aspen. The thickness, higher pH value, scarring, and high level of nutrients contained in aged aspen bark creates an ideal microenvironment for lichen.

Xanthoria parietina lichen, also known as maritime sunburst lichen, is one of the most common lichen species found in hardwood forests in the Pacific Northwest. The vegetative body of the lichen is foliose in form, which means that it has leaf-like structures, and its shape is lobed, or round. The upper surface is often a bright, cheerful yellow, but it can also be orange or a yellowish green. While it does grow on rocks, it's most often seen growing in humid microclimates on hardwood trees or bark, such as aged aspen.

Good to Know

Quaking aspen's scientific name is *Populus tremuloides*. The name *tremuloides* is derived from the Latin word *tremulus*, which means "to tremble."

AGED ASPEN BARK

The following process will give you tremendous insight as to how far you can take the metal by both heating and forming. I encourage you to let go of any expectations you may have because the results will undoubtedly be different than anticipated. They will surprise and delight you. Given that the aspen's smooth silvery greenish-white bark becomes furrowed with age, this will allow you much room for trial and happy accidents. Try to relax, breathe, and watch closely as the silver comes to life.

Tools and Materials

Smith Little Torch Propane and Oxygen System with #7 torch tip

Silquar Soldering Board

22-gauge sterling silver sheet

24-gauge sterling silver sheet

2' (61 cm) 16-gauge sterling silver wire, cut into 4" (10 cm) lengths

Cross locking tweezers

Separating disc

Flex shaft or high-speed Dremel Rotary Tool

Cross cut cylinder bur (optional)

GreenLion Saw Frame

3/0 saw blade

Bench pin

Eastern Repoussé and Chasing Tools Set

Fretz Chasing Hammer

Anvil or steel bench block

Ball bur, various sizes

Round-nose pliers

AdvantEdge burs, varying shapes and sizes

Black silicone polishing disc

2 third hand tools

Silver dust (optional)

Titanium pick

Copper tongs

Rawhide or nylon mallet

Bracelet mandrel (optional)

My-T-Flux or similar liquid hard-soldering flux

Easy, medium, and hard solder

Extra easy solder (optional)

Liver of sulfur, dry concentrate

Fine fiber wheel

Mild soap and water

Techniques

This tutorial is broken down into three parts.

Part 1. The Creation of the Bark Underlayer

Fusing

Reticulation

Forming with repoussé chasing tools

Part 2. The Creation of the Bark Overlayer

Fusing

Forming with repoussé chasing tools

Texturing with flex shaft

Part 3. Soldering the Layers Together

Soldering multiple layers of sheet together

Pick soldering

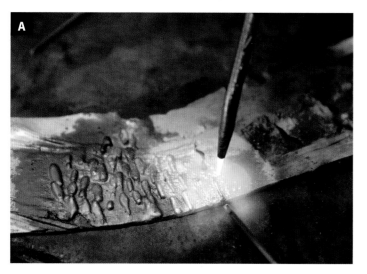

Part 1. The Creation of the Bark Underlayer

1. You may choose to create a cuff, ring, or something else. Whatever the case, what you make will determine the dimensions of your 22- and 24-gauge sheets. Place the 22-gauge sheet on your soldering platform. Set several pieces of the 16-gauge wire on your platform so that you do not need to turn your torch on and off as you work.

2. Hold a piece of 16-gauge wire in cross locking tweezers. Consistently heat the sheet, watching the color change from gray to black. As soon as it turns red and one spot begins to quiver and molten, set the tip of the wire on top to fuse. As the wire slumps beneath the heat, continue to heat the mass (silver sheet) as you follow the slumping wire with your torch. [A, B]

3. When you have neared the end of the wire, fuse it to one of the spare pieces of wire on your soldering platform.

   Continue to fuse to the sheet before it cools. If the wire balls or splits as you're fusing, you're not sufficiently heating the sheet. Return to those areas and heat the sheet until the wire is absorbed and fuses.

4. You can try the following exercises to understand how far you can work the metal with your torch:

   • Hold your torch in one place until you burn a hole all the way through the sheet.

   • Patch the hole, fusing wire to the sheet on either side of the hole.

   • Hold your torch in one place until you almost burn a hole in the sheet. This technique will add to the mottled appearance and blend the wire more thoroughly into the sheet.

   • Steadily hold your torch on the edge of your sheet. As soon as the edge begins to reticulate, slowly move in one direction to reticulate an entire section.

   Anneal the piece. Pickle and quench. [C]

5. On the bottom side of the formed sheet, you may choose to add a scratched, string-like texture. To do this, use the separating disc to carve consistent linear lines in one direction across the surface of the silver. [D]

   You can also use a small cross cut cylinder bur to carve out patterns or accentuate the textures. Save the silver dust! [E]

Part 2. The Creation of the Bark Overlayer

6. Saw the 24-gauge sheet into a patchwork-type puzzle. Saw inward to create intentional tears in the bark.

7. Place the puzzle pieces on your soldering platform. Set several pieces of the 16-gauge wire on your soldering platform. [F]

8. Repeat steps 2 and 3 above. [G, H]

   Anneal, pickle, and quench.

continued on next page

9. With both the small and large planishing tools, add form between each section of fused wire. As you hammer, drag the tool rather than lift. Turn your piece over to form around your work on the other side, causing the sheet to undulate. [I]

    Watch the color because you may have to anneal so that it doesn't become too brittle and crack.

10. With round-nose pliers, gently twist the silver to give it more dimension. [J]

11. Use an AdvantEdge bur to remove unwanted marring. This will also give the metal a velvety finish that resembles the photosynthesized outer layer of aspen bark. Soften the edges with the black silicone polishing disc. [K]

    Anneal, pickle, and quench.

12. You can taper the edges with the separating disc. [L]

13. Add some texture with a ball bur. [M]

14. Place the entire piece in water. While wet, sprinkle a thin layer of silver dust in chosen areas. [N]

    Place the piece in a third hand. Heat from below and watch as the silver dust turns from white to yellow, gold, and black.

    As soon as the silver dust turns black, support the underside with your pick and heat from above.

15. Slowly move your torch in concentrated circular motions as the metal turns red and the silver dust stops glowing. Then, anneal, quench, and set aside. [O]

Part 3. Soldering the Layers Together

16. If you have chosen to fabricate a cuff or ring, use a rawhide or nylon mallet to hammer the bark underlayer into the appropriate form. I use my anvil or a bracelet mandrel to form my cuffs. [P]

    The overlayer can be bent with your fingers and doesn't need to be 100% flush with the underlayer. However, it must meet in 2 or more spots where it can be soldered.

continued on next spread

Good to Know

Lenticels, a.k.a. breathing holes, allow the exchange of oxygen and carbon dioxide between the atmosphere and the living cells of trees. When aspen bark ages, the diamond-shaped lenticels become less defined, more mottled. To make these, use various sizes of ball burs to scar the metal.

17. Each piece of the bark overlayer puzzle will be soldered onto the underlayer one at a time. You'll begin at one end of the puzzle with hard solder, transition to medium, and finish with easy solder at the other. To hold the pieces in place, use the third hands. Flux the entire surface. [Q]

18. Place several pieces of hard solder on your soldering platform. Pick up a piece of solder with your pick and then turn your torch to your piece. [R]

19. Consistently heat the entire piece until the color of the mass turns from white to a dull yellow. Pick the solder to each point of contact. [S]

Continue heating the entire piece while also focusing your torch in a spot where it will coax the silver in the direction of contact. Continue to heat the entire mass until all solder has flowed. When the silver has oxidized, STOP. Pickle and quench.

20. Repeat steps 14 and 15 with medium and easy solder. You can use the second third hand as a heat sink to prevent previous solder joints from reflowing.

21. When every puzzle piece is securely soldered onto the underlayer, pickle and quench. Patina with liver of sulfur. Brush off some of the patina with a fine fiber wheel.

22. Wash with water and mild soap. To turn the outer bark layer a little more white, place your piece back in the pickle for 2 to 5 minutes.

Soldering: Pick Tips

To pick solder effectively, keep two things in mind: a clean pick and a cool pick. Clean your pick with files or sandpaper. Heat the solder, not your pick. If your pick is hot, the solder will stick to the soldering platform. Quench your pick and try again.

XANTHORIA PARIETINA LICHEN

Tools and Materials

Smith Little Torch Propane and Oxygen System with #6 and #7 torch tip

Silquar Soldering Board

Sterling silver scraps

3" (7.6 cm) 16-gauge sterling silver wire (optional)

Cross locking tweezers

Container (i.e., bucket) with cold water

Disc cutter

Brass hammer

Anvil or steel bench block

Dapping set with block

Titanium pick

Copper tongs

Hard, medium, and easy solder

Bale or brooch fastener (optional)

Techniques

Water casting

Sweat soldering

Pick soldering

Soldering wire through hole in sheet (optional)

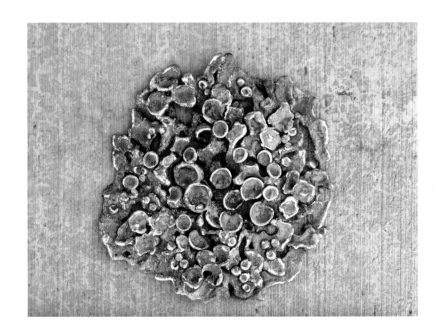

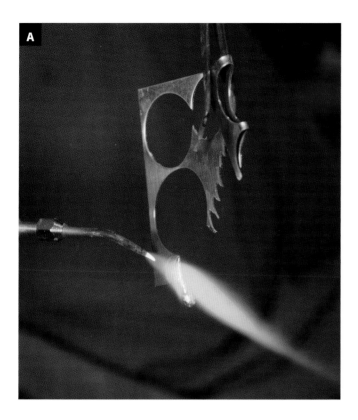

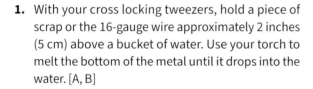

1. With your cross locking tweezers, hold a piece of scrap or the 16-gauge wire approximately 2 inches (5 cm) above a bucket of water. Use your torch to melt the bottom of the metal until it drops into the water. [A, B]

2. Punch out as many circles as you choose with the disc cutter. Anneal, pickle, and quench.

3. Hammer the discs into cups with a dapping block.

4. With the cups sitting upright on your soldering platform, use your torch to gently reticulate the edges. Make sure that your torch is pointing across the rim rather than down so that the cup doesn't warp. Set them aside. [C]

5. Reticulate the edges of scrap silver pieces. If you're worried about the edges drawing inward, use your pick as a heat sink. Quench or let cool to room temperature.

   Anneal, pickle, and quench. Remember that a high heat actually hardens your silver, so it's important to anneal before forming. [D, E]

continued on next page

6. For the lichen pictured, I soldered the components together starting from the lobes, the outside of the form, working inward toward the fungal fruiting bodies, called apothecia, which are the bodies that contain the spores.

   My rationale in doing so was that it would be easier to solder the smaller components (steps 1 and 2) to the larger mass (step 5) without impacting the multitude of solder joints at the center of the piece. In addition, this allowed me to first determine the size of the piece and fill in empty spaces as I worked inward.

   To begin, arrange all of the reticulated edges into a circle with two separate piles of water castings and reticulated cups on the side. [F]

7. Change to a #7 torch tip. Ensure that the pressure reading on your tanks matches the number on your torch tip (7).

8. Fuse as many of the outer components together as possible. Watch the color of the metal to be sure that each of the components is reaching the exact same melting temperature (red) at the exact same time. [G]

9. Once each of the reticulated edges is fused, you can further round them out by pointing your torch directly at an edge until it begins to curl upward. [H]

10. Fuse a few of the reticulated cups to the piece. As you do this, focus your torch on the mass and use your pick as a heat sink to protect the smaller components from melting until they simultaneously reach the melting point. [I]

11. You'll notice that fusing becomes more challenging as your mass increases, and you may lose some detail. At this point, switch to solder. Pickle and quench the piece.

When you switch to solder, begin with hard. Continue to use your pick to protect the smaller components as they are being added. Be sure to heat the mass sufficiently for the solder to flow. [J]

12. You'll eventually switch to medium solder as you fill in empty spaces. The goal is for the lichen to appear as if it's spreading across the surface. [K]

13. To help you envision where you might take this piece, I torch fired enamel across the surface of the piece to depict the actual lichen more accurately. [L]

14. Use easy solder to attach a bale or brooch fastener on the back side of the piece.

Good to Know

The outer surface of Xanthoria parietina lichen is the *cortex*, the middle fluffy fungal layer is the *medulla*, and the holdfasts (if it has any) are called *rhizines*. The colorful pigments are all in the cortex and are for UV protection. There are some lichens associated with green algae, some with green algae plus cyanobacteria (or blue-green algae), and a very few with just cyanobacteria. They're also associated with spores from basidiomycetes (the mushrooms!).

Clamshell with Barnacles

WE SPENT A LONG WEEKEND CAMPING AT PORT BLAKELY at the northern-most tip of Washington state. Our daily ritual was to take long beach walks, kayak, throw sticks out into the harbor for our dogs, and watch the heron fish before sunset. It was during one of these moments that I looked down to see a large clamshell covered with barnacles, bleached white from the sun. I picked it up, and as I turned it over in my hands, I wondered as I often do, "How can I make this?" Back in my studio, I experimented with new techniques to fabricate the shell and barnacles. I also did my due diligence to research and learn about their important roles in keeping nature's balance.

The hard clam is both ecologically and economically important. It's commercially harvested for sale and consumption, and it plays a significant role in recycling organic material to maintain clean water. As a filter feeder, it uses a set of siphons for respiration and feeding on algae. It can filter up to 1 gallon (3.8 L) of water per hour.

As a member of the crustacean family, barnacles begin life as fertilized, floating eggs. They cement themselves to suitable substrates and spend their entire adult life in the same place, standing on their heads, kicking their legs out of their shell to catch their food. Barnacles are suspension feeders, consuming plankton and dissolved detritus suspended in seawater and are therefore essential in cleansing that water for other organisms. They are also a food source for these animals. Because of their filtration feeding method, barnacles are extremely vulnerable to pollution, particularly plastic microparticles, as is the entire marine ecosystem.

Like many shelled organisms, barnacles and their colonies are subject to many threats including ship groundings, damage from marine construction and debris, and ocean acidification, a process that threatens their ability to produce and maintain their calcium carbonate skeleton.

We can all do our part to protect and preserve these animals and the ecosystems that rely on them by doing the following:

Reducing our use of plastics.

Using less energy.

Choosing sustainable seafood.

Supporting policies that support invertebrate conservation, habitat restoration, and water quality.

Consider using a nontoxic foul-release coating for boats.

Here's something to ponder. The next time you're walking across barnacle-covered rocks while exploring enticing tide pools, remember that the barnacles are *alive*. Tread carefully.

Tools and Materials

Smith Little Torch Propane and Oxygen System with #6 torch tip

Silquar Soldering Board

Sterling silver sheet, 3" x 3" (7.6 x 7.6 cm), 22 gauge

16-gauge sterling silver wire

Pencil or Sharpie Permanent Marker, Ultra Fine Point

GreenLion Saw Frame

3/0 saw blade

Bench pin

Fretz Set #3 H-2 Micro Stake Set

Bench vise

Rawhide mallet

Cross locking tweezers

Carbide cone bur

Flex shaft or high-speed Dremel Rotary Tool

Cross cut cylinder bur

Diamond knife edge bur

Separating disc

Flush cutters

Titanium pick

Copper tongs

My-T-Flux or similar liquid hard-soldering flux

Hard, medium, and easy solder

Black silicone polishing disc

Ball bur (small enough to fit inside tiny barnacles, but no specific size required)

Fine and coarse fiber wheels (optional)

Techniques

Sawing

Forming with stakes

Fusing

Carving and texturing with flex shaft

Soldering to both sides of sheet

1. Trace the outline of an actual clamshell onto the sheet of silver. Saw around the outline of the template. Anneal, pickle, and quench. [A]

2. Place the Fretz M-9 Miniature High-Dome Mushroom Bezel-Forming Stake in its holder and mount it in your vise.

   Your goal is to mimic the shape of the shell, so keep the actual shell handy to continuously ensure that your forming work is heading in the right direction. [B]

   With your mallet, begin forming the sheet over the stake, starting from the outside of the sheet, working toward the center. Be consistent with your hammering to achieve a smoother form rather than one that is dimpled. [C]

   Repeat this step 4 to 5 times, re-annealing each time it becomes gray and brittle.

3. To form the less domed ventral slope of the shell, switch to the Fretz M-8 Miniature Low-Dome Mushroom Bezel-Forming Stake. Continue to anneal as needed.

4. As you work toward the high plate and umbo, where the two halves of the clamshell are hinged together and the curve of the shell intensifies, switch to the Fretz M-6 Miniature High-Dome Mushroom Bezel-Forming Stake. [D]

   You'll even switch to the Miniature Micro-Mushroom Bezel-Forming Stakes, although you may want to wait until step 7.

5. Periodically place your silver shell upside down on a surface to ensure that the edges sit flat. Continue forming if they're still wonky.When you're happy with the basic shape of the shell, turn it over on your soldering platform, cup facing upward, to work on the hinge.

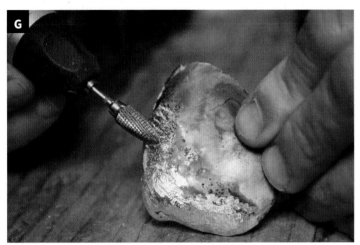

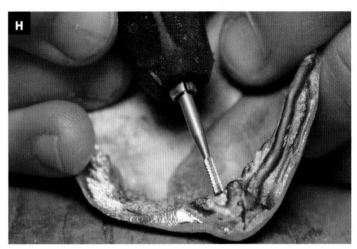

Place a 3- to 4-inch (7.6 to 10 cm) length of 16-gauge wire in your cross locking tweezers. Heat the shell (the mass). When the sheet turns red and molten, lay the wire alongside the upper edge of the sheet until it fuses.

Heat the mass more than the wire. The two pieces of metal must reach the exact same temperature (melting point) at the exact same time in order to fuse.

If your wire "clumps" or breaks apart and balls on top of your sheet, that means you're heating the wire more than the mass. Instead, focus your flame directly IN FRONT of the wire, ON THE MASS, and the two should fuse almost seamlessly. [E]

6. Use the Miniature Micro-Mushroom Bezel-Forming Stakes to accentuate the umbo. [F]

7. Use the carbide cone bur to shave off any extra or unwanted bumps or blemishes. [G]

Use a smaller cross cut cylinder bur to carve out the hinge teeth. [H]

continued on next page

Scan to watch
a video tutorial

8. Switch to a diamond knife edge bur to fine-tune the hinge and outer edge of the shell. [I]

9. With a slightly firmer grip and sufficient pressure so that the texture doesn't disappear when polishing, use the separating disc to add the bivalves. [J]

10. To make barnacles, with flush cutters, snip small pieces of silver scrap (wire or sheet will do) and place them across your soldering platform. As you heat each piece of silver, stick your pick into it. [K, L]

11. Flux the entire surface of your shell and place the barnacles inside in "growing" groups. Place hard solder in between the barnacles. Heat the shell from below to draw the solder beneath the barnacles. [M, N]

12. On the top side of the shell, repeat the prior step, this time using medium solder.

13. Use the black silicone polishing disc to clean up unwanted solder puddles and to re-apply texture to the shell.

14. Use a small ball bur to accentuate the inside of each barnacle. [O]

15. Use the black silicone polishing disc to sand down any rough edges. [P]

16. Finish as desired.

Good to Know

Bivalves (mollusks with a hinged shell) are similar to trees in that you can determine their age by counting the number of growth lines on their shells, just as you would count the rings of a tree trunk.

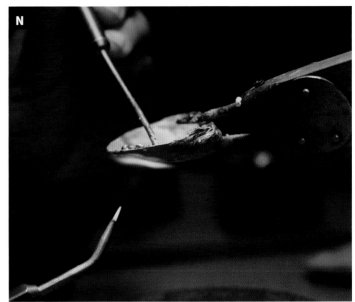

Kinetic Luna Moth

THE LUNA MOTH (*ACTIAS LUNA*) IS ONE OF THE LARGEST SPECIES OF MOTHS IN NORTH AMERICA, with a wingspan of 3 to 4 inches (7.5 to 10 cm). It inhabits deciduous forests, where its vibrant green wings blend in among the leaves.

Adult luna moths have no mouths and do not feed. Their sole purpose is to reproduce, and they die after only one week. During that time they survive on stored fat from their larval stage.

Adult females lay their eggs on the leaves of their host plants, including sweet gum, hickory, sumac, walnut, and white birch trees. After about one week, the caterpillars hatch and begin a month-long eating binge, shedding their skin four times to accommodate their growth.

When it's full grown, the caterpillar uses silk and leaves to spin a cocoon. The following autumn, the adult luna moth emerges from the cocoon and expands and dries its wings, beginning the ancient cycle again.

The female luna moth releases a pheromone that males detect with their comb-like antennae. Mating takes place after midnight, and the female begins laying eggs the following evening, which continues for several nights.

Since they do not feed, adult luna moths do not pollinate like other moth species. Instead, they provide food for bats, owls, and the nocturnal whippoorwill. Interestingly, their long twisted hind wings scatter reflected sounds that confuse the echolocation hunting method of bats.

Tools and Materials

Smith Little Torch Propane and Oxygen System with #6 torch tip

Silquar Soldering Board

Sterling silver sheet, 3" x 3" (7.6 x 7.6 cm), 22-gauge

16-gauge sterling silver wire

21-gauge sterling silver wire

Recycled sterling silver buttons

Copper, brass, or gold wire (optional)

GreenLion Saw Frame

3/0 saw blade

Bench pin

Hard, medium, and easy solder

Separating disc

Eastern Repoussé and Chasing Tools Set

Fretz Chasing Hammer

Anvil or steel bench block

Titanium pick

Copper tongs

Sharpie Permanent Marker, Ultra Fine Point

Round-nose pliers

Cross cut cylinder bur

Round burs

Flex shaft or high-speed Dremel Rotary Tool

Drill bit for 16-gauge wire

Flush cutters

Third hand tool (optional)

My-T-Flux or similar liquid hard-soldering flux

Bale (optional)

Cross locking tweezers

Fine and coarse fiber wheels (optional)

Techniques

Sawing

Texturing with repoussé and chasing tools

Fusing

Carving and texturing with flex shaft

Soldering to fused form

Hand fabricated hinge

---

1. Transfer an image of luna moth wings to the 22-gauge sterling silver sheet. Saw them out. Anneal, pickle, and quench.

   Note. You'll want to connect the wings diagonally. [A]

   continued on next page

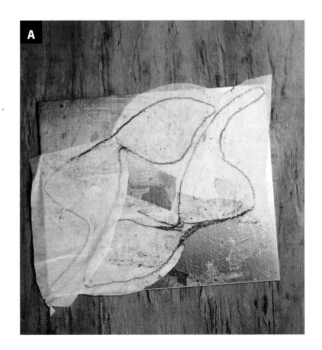

2. To create the coastal margins on the upper forewing pair, place 16-gauge wire along the back edge.

   Place 4 small pieces of easy solder alongside the wire. Like step 9 in fabricating a leaf, heat the wire directly across from each solder bit. Turn up your torch and focus the heat on the mass until your solder runs the entire length beneath the wire. Pickle and quench. [B]

3. For the coastal margins on the upper forewing pair, turn the wings over and place 16-gauge wire along the top edge. Repeat step 2.

   Blend the wire into the wings with the separating disc.

4. Use the large chasing and repoussé line tool to consistently add texture across the entire wingspan, on the same sides that you soldered the wire. [C]

5. You'll likely need to anneal the metal before continuing. Then, carefully fold the wings over round nose pliers so that the textured sides are both face forward. Set aside. [D]

6. *Optional step.* You can use copper, brass, or gold to solder on the luna moth's distinguishing eyespots. Pickle and quench. [E]

7. Saw out the shape of the feathered antennae. [F]

8. Fold a 1-inch (2.5 cm) piece of 21-gauge wire at a 4-degree angle. Fuse a ½-inch (1.3 cm) piece of 16-gauge wire to the bottom to create a *Y*. [G]

9. Sweat the *Y* to the sawed antennae sheet, allowing the 16-gauge wire to act as a pin. DO NOT snip off the excess. Pickle and quench. [H]

continued on next spread

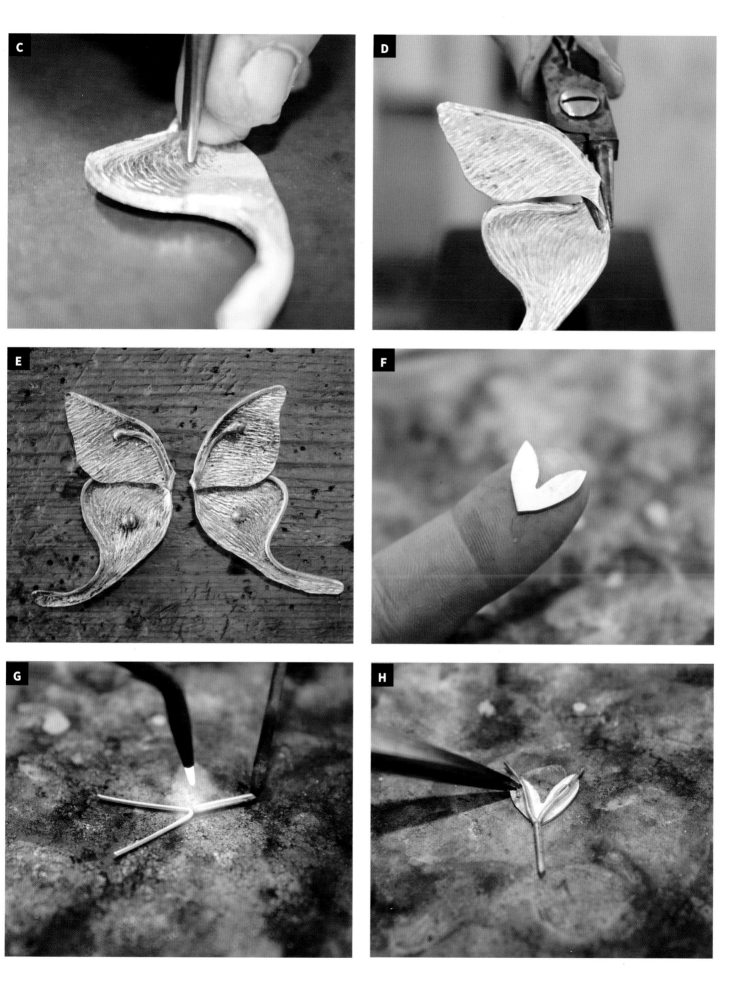

10. Use the separating disc to blend the wire into the sheet. Saw out the feather-like pattern on the antennae and set aside. [I, J]

11. For this next step, I usually fuse the abdomen, thorax, and eyes into one mass, and then I carve out the details. Fortunately, with the luna moth's fuzzy body, its features are less distinctive. It's important to note, however, that you'll be carving deep grooves in the body to create room for hinges, so it needs to have sufficient girth to do so.

    Arrange melted buttons in the general shape of the moth body. Begin heating the center of the mass. When your silver buttons soft fuse together, move your torch outward to the edges. Log roll the body as you heat so that it doesn't adhere to the soldering platform. [K]

    As you did with the dragonfly body (see page 108), use the tip of your pick as a heat sink to prevent the abdomen from shrinking. [L]

    Continue to log roll the form to redistribute mass as needed and to round out each side. Add more material if needed and use the heat of your torch to redistribute mass.

12. Hold the wings up against the moth body and use a Sharpie to mark the mass that you'll need to carve from the thorax. Leave enough room to keep a partition between the wings. [M]

13. As you carve, make sure you hold the body with pliers because the metal will get hot. Begin with a cross cut cylinder bur to carve a notch on each side. Your goal is for each of the wing pairs to sit flush on each side of the thorax. [N]

14. Switch to a round bur to deepen each notch, as well as to round them out, allowing the wings to pivot seamlessly. The wings should fit like a puzzle no matter whether they're lying flat or pivoted upward. [O, P]

continued on next spread

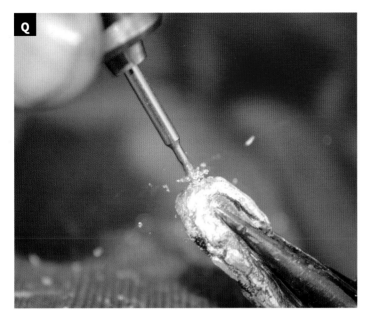

15. Drill a hole into the top of the moth's head for the antennae. [Q]

16. Use the Sharpie once again to mark the top and bottom of the wing pairs, immediately above and below where they connect to the thorax.

    Drill two holes through the partition. [R]

17. Fit the antennae into the top of the moth and sweat hard solder to the bottom of the antennae. Heat the mass to coax the solder into the hole. [S, T]

18. Thread a 1-inch (2.5 cm) piece of 16-gauge wire through one wing pair and fold it at a 90-degree angle on each end. [U]

19. Feed the wire through the holes in the partition. With flush cutters, snip the bottom wire so that it protrudes only ⅛ inch (3 mm). Bend the upper wire into a 90-degree angle and feed in through the second wing pair. Snip the upper wire where it connects with the bottom wire. [V]

20. Ensure that the wires are touching one another but NEITHER the wings NOR the thorax. Use a third hand if you need to hold the wings at an angle for an adequate setup. Sometimes, I even have my third hands clamping cross locking tweezers to create different angles while holding my work. Flux and pick medium solder to the wire tips. Pickle and quench. [W]

21. You can use a smaller cross cut cylinder bur to add a fluffy-like texture to the moth's body.

22. I often add a bale on the back side of the moth's body or include it in an intricate ring bowl. Use easy solder to do so. Finish as desired. [X]

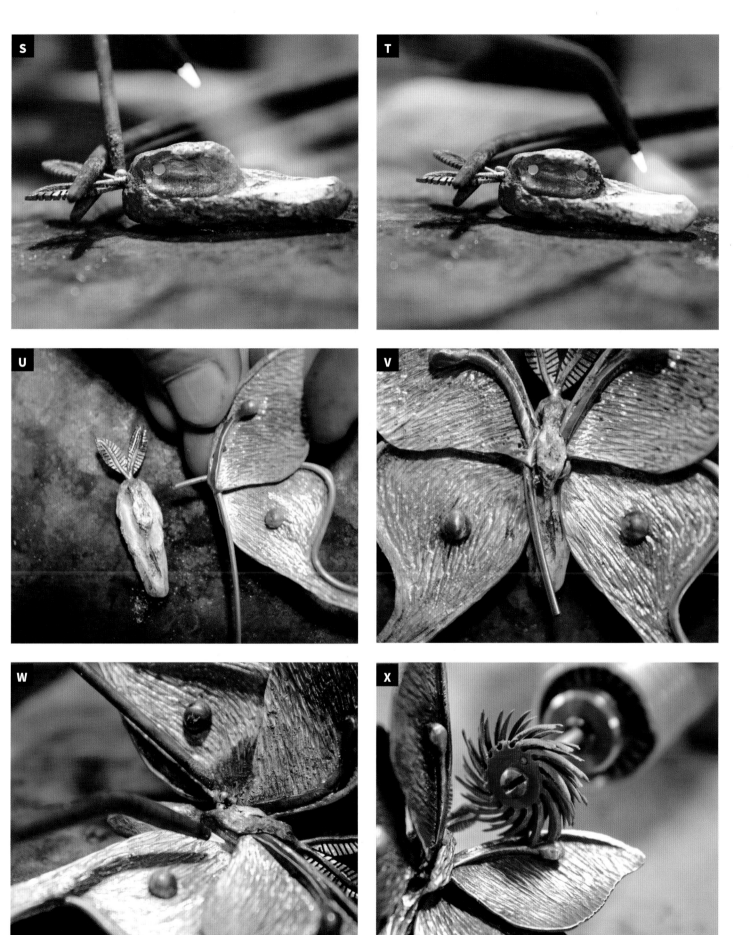

Steps for Finishing Your Work

AS YOU HAVE SEEN THROUGHOUT THIS BOOK, I tend to work differently than other metalsmiths. The same goes for finishing my work. Many use magnetic tumblers to polish, and some claim that tumbling helps to work-harden their pieces. Personally, I've found that work-hardening is best done with a hammer and by gently twisting the metal (such as ear wires). Once my pieces are work-hardened, I follow the steps outlined below to finish.

Tools and Materials

Smith Little Torch Propane and Oxygen System

Silquar Soldering Board

Flex shaft or high-speed Dremel Rotary Tool

Separating disc

Black silicone polishing disc

Fiber wheels, coarse, medium, or fine

Warm water

Liver of sulfur, dry concentrate

Flux brush

Baking soda

Dedeco Sunburst Radial Discs

Cotton polishing wheel with compound rouge

Mild hand soap

1. In the flex shaft, use the separating disc followed by a black silicone polishing disc to remove excess solder and sharp edges or points. [A, B]

   I sometimes brush the silver with a coarse fiber wheel, which allows it to absorb the liver of sulfur (LOS) more effectively in the next step.

   Rinse off the dust and debris with warm water.

2. There are many ways to prepare LOS. Some place the LOS in a warm crock pot, which works quickly, but unfortunately only lasts one day. Instead, I place a few LOS chips in a mason jar and mix it with room temperature water. Then, as I heat the piece, I use a small paint brush to dip into the LOS mixture and paint on the piece. When finished, I cover the mason jar, and it lasts for up to one week. [C]

3. **Note.** The flame should be an annealing flame. You do not need to heat the piece to solder-melting point. It merely needs to be just warm enough for the LOS to be effective.

   Here's an interesting side note: Before using LOS, I used hard boiled eggs to oxidize my pieces. To do so, I placed warm hardboiled eggs, shells included, in sealed Ziplock bags, crushed them with my hands, and then placed my piece in the middle of the crushed eggs. It took about 24 hours for the silver to oxidize.

4. To stop the LOS oxidization process, rinse your piece in a mixture of baking soda and water.

   Then, rinse with water.

continued on next page

5. You can use coarse, medium, and fine fiber wheels to remove some of the LOS from your piece. This will give the silver a shadowy contrast. [D]

6. Continue to remove the LOS with a Dedeco Sunburst Radial Disc. You will see that these discs also polish the silver. [E]

7. At this point, you may choose to further polish your piece with a polishing wheel and rouge. This step is not necessary, but I like how the high sheen contrasts with the darker LOS hues. Be sure to wear safety glasses and a respiratory mask. Lightly add rouge to the polishing wheel as it's turning and then press your piece against the wheel. [F]

8. Thoroughly wash your piece with soap and water. [G]

Notes

These endnotes are presented in order of their appearance in the projects.

Salmon, page 96

"Their perilous, exhausting annual journey . . . ." National Geographic: www.nationalgeographic.com/animals/fish/facts/salmon

"Unfortunately, sockeye salmon are vulnerable . . . ." NOAA Fisheries: www.fisheries.noaa.gov/species/sockeye-salmon-protected

"Since each part of a salmon's life cycle . . . ." Pacific Wild: https://pacificwild.org/salmon-a-keystone-species/

"Here are just a few things we can do to help . . . ." State of Salmon: https://stateofsalmon.wa.gov/how-to-help/

Ode to a Dragonfly, page 106

"Their decline is the result . . . ." National Geographic: www.nationalgeographic.com/animals/invertebrates/facts/dragonflies-insects

"Here are just a few ways that we can help . . . ." ScienceDirect: www.sciencedirect.com/topics/earth-and-planetary-sciences/dragonfly

A Migrating Monarch Butterfly, page 116

"This is one of the world's longest insect migrations." World Wildlife Fund: www.worldwildlife.org/species/monarch-butterfly

"Unfortunately, the migratory monarch butterfly has decreased . . . ." WWF Monitoring Reports: www.worldwildlife.org/publications/areas-of-forest-occupied-by-the-colonies-of-monarch-butterflies-in-mexico-during-the-2021-2022-overwintering-period

"Here are just a few ways that we can help . . . ." The Conservation Foundation: www.theconservationfoundation.org/monarch-butterflies-are-endangered-heres-how-you-can-help/

Aged Aspen Bark and Lichen, page 124

"The thickness, higher pH value, ..." https://digitalcommons.usu.edu/aspen_bib/

Xanthoria Parietina Lichen, page 132

"Good to Know" fact provided by my dear friend Peter Neitlich, Lichenologist for the National Park Service Alaska Region's Natural Resources Team and Inventory and Monitoring Program.

Clamshell with Barnacles, page 136

"It can filter up to . . . ." NOAA Fisheries: www.fisheries.noaa.gov

"Because of their filtration feeding method . . . ." National Ocean Service: https://oceanservice.noaa.gov

"Like many shelled organisms . . . ." National Marine Sanctuary Foundation: https://marinesanctuary.org

Kinetic Luna Moth, page 142

"Interestingly, their long twisted hind wings . . . ." Missouri Department of Conservation: https://mdc.mo.gov/discover-nature/field-guide/luna-moth

Glossary

Annealing. A heat-treatment process used to increase the ductility and reduce the hardness of a material; it is done after the metal has undergone a hardening process to prevent it from being brittle and for further forming.

Back plate. The sheet of silver that is in the back or forms a back of a jewelry piece.

Bale (also spelled "bail"). A component of certain types of jewelry, mostly necklaces, that is used to attach a pendant or stone.

Button. Sterling silver scraps melted into the shape of a domed disc.

Copper alloys. Metal alloys that have copper as their principal component.

Dapping. The process of turning a piece of flat metal into a domed shape by molding it into some sort of depression within a wood or metal block.

Drilling. A cutting process where a drill bit is spun to cut a hole of circular cross-section in a solid material.

Fire scale. A topical discoloration of black scale on the surface of silver; it is cleaned with pickle, which dissolves it.

Fire stain. A layer of oxides that is visible on the surface of objects made of metal alloys containing copper when the object is heated; on copper-containing alloys of gold or of silver (such as sterling silver), it presents as a red or purple stain; the only way to remove fire stain is to grind or etch it out.

Flush fit. When two or more sides of metal fit together precisely without gaps.

Forging. A metal working process that manipulates, shapes, and compresses metal to achieve a desired form; the forging process can be completed using either hot or cold forging processes.

Forming. Involves the reshaping of metals while still in the solid state, accomplished without the use of heat.

Fusing. The use of heat to join multiple pieces of metal into one without the use of solder.

Gauge. A number designation related to the thickness and weight per square foot of the metal; gauges for sheet metal range from 30 to 1, with a higher number indicating a thinner piece of material.

Gray. The color of sterling silver when it is dirty, hard, non-porous, and brittle.

Hard fuse. The use of heat to join multiple pieces of metal into one without the use of solder, when the definition between pieces can no longer be identified.

Heat sink. A component that increases the heat flow away from a hot device.

Heating from above. Directing the heat of your torch on top of the piece.

Heating from below. Directing the heat of your torch below the piece, thereby protecting the upper layers or details.

Hollow form. A curved or concave form with a cavity, gap, or space within.

Log rolling. Using a pick or other probing instrument to roll a fused form across the soldering platform before while the outer layer has reached its melting point and the interior remains solid.

Marring the metal. Any disfigurement, blemish, discoloration, weathering or stretching, or the like, that alters the physical appearance of the metal.

Mass. The more metal there is, the longer it will take to heat.

Melting point. The moment the metal transitions from a solid phase into a liquid phase.

Molten. When the metal has been heated to a very high temperature and has become a hot, thick liquid.

Neutralizing pickle. Adding a base, usually baking soda, to neutralize the used pickle before disposing of it.

Oxidization. When the outer surface of the metal has been darkened via a chemical process, speeding up the natural tarnishing process, creating a dark patina which consists of a layer of silver sulfide.

Pick soldering. Utilizing a pick to transfer solder from the soldering platform to the piece.

Piercing. A shearing process in which raw metal is pierced with a machining tool, such as a twist drill, resulting in the creation of a circular or other shaped hole.

Pinhole. A small hole in a hollow form that relieves pressure when soldering the components together.

Puddling. Heating solder until it puddles.

Quench. The rapid cooling of metal to adjust the mechanical properties of its original state.

Red. The melting point of metal.

Repoussé. A French word that means "pushed back," referring to any type of ornamentation in which the design is raised in relief on the reverse or interior side of the metal.

Reticulation. A pattern or arrangement of interlacing lines resembling a net; a decorative surface finishing technique involving the application of localized heat to the surface of a metal.

Silver dust. The metal shards left over from carving and filing, to be used for fusing textures onto pieces.

Slumping. Heating the metal until it slumps or drapes.

Soft fuse. The use of heat to join multiple pieces of metal into one without the use of solder, when the definition between pieces is still visible.

Solder flow point. When the metal has reached the solder's melting point; hard silver solder melts at approximately 1365°F (740°C), medium at 1275°F (690°C), easy at 1240°F (671°C); the color of the metal will turn a dull yellow hue just before the solder has reached its melting point.

Soldering. A joining process used to join different types of metals together by melting solder.

Sweat soldering. A process of joining two metals together by puddling the solder on one surface before joining the second surface and reheating to form a joint.

Tapering. To reduce in thickness toward one end.

White. The color of sterling silver when it is annealed and pickled; it is clean and malleable.

Work hardening. Increase in hardness of a metal, induced, deliberately or accidentally, by hammering, rolling, drawing, or other physical processes; it can also occur when the metal is overheated.

Yellow. The color of sterling silver when it is annealed, pickled, fluxed, and heated to the temperature just before the solder has reached its melting point.

Resources

Associations

American Gem Society (AGS): americangemsociety.org

American Gem Trade Association (AGTA): agta.org

American Jewelry Design Council (AJDC): ajdc.org

Jewelers of America (JA) : jewelers.org

Metalsmith Society: metalsmithsociety.com

Women's Jewelry Association (WJA): womensjewelryassociation.com

For additional listings, visit: jewelspan.com/jewel-span-resources.php?resource=Associations

Books

Bolton, Corkie. *Metalsmith Society's Guide to Jewelry Making.* Salem, MA: Page Street Publishing, 2022.

Bone, Elizabeth. *Silversmithing for Jewellery Makers.* Turnbridge Wells, Kent, UK: Search Press, 2022.

Caines, Jeanette K. *Soldering Demystified.* New York, NY: self-published, 2015.

Corwin, Nancy Megan. *Chasing and Repoussé.* Brunswick, ME: Brynmorgen Press, 2009.

Darty, Linda. *The Art of Enameling.* New York, NY: Union Square & Co., 2006.

de Waard, Machi, and Janet Richardson. *Silver Jewellery Making.* Turnbridge Wells, Kent, UK: Search Press, 2021.

Dhein, Christine. *Eco Jewelry Handbook.* Brunswick, ME: Brynmorgen Press, 2018.

Fettolini, Jose Luis. *Sustainable Jewellery, Updated Edition.* Barcelona, Spain: Hoaki, 2022.

McCreight, Tim. *Complete Metalsmith: Professional Edition.* Brunswick, ME: Brynmorgen Press, 2005.

McGrath, Jinks. *Metalsmithing for Jewelry Makers.* Naperville, IL: B.E.S. Publishing, 2013.

Revere, Alan. *Professional Jewelry Making.* Brunswick, ME: Brynmorgen Press, 2011.

Richbourg, Kate. *Metalsmithing Made Easy.* Iola, WI: Krause Craft, 2016.

Richbourg, Kate Ferrant. *Simple Soldering.* Iola, WI: Krause Craft, 2012.

Shapiro, Emilie. *How to Create Your Own Jewelry Line.* New York, NY: Union Square $ Co., 2016.

Silvera, Joe. *Soldering Made Simple.* Waukesha, WI: Kalmbach Books, 2010.

Young, Anastasia. *The Workbench Guide to Jewelry Techniques.* Loveland, CO: Interweave, 2010.

Magazines

American Craft: craftcouncil.org/magazine/american-craft

Art Jewelry: no longer in publication; back issues may be found in libraries or purchased online

Bead&Button: no longer in publication; back issues may be found in libraries or purchased online

Belle Armoire Jewelry Magazine: stampington.com/belle-armoire-jewelry

National Jeweler: nationaljeweler.com/magazines

Ornament: ornamentmagazine.org/about

Podcasts

For the Love of Jewelers: riogrande.com/for-the-love-of-jewelers

Jewelry Artist: interweave.com/category/jewelry-artist-podcast

Jewellers Academy: jewellersacademy.com/podcast

Slowmade: christinemighion.com/pages/slowmade-podcast

The Jewelry District: jckonline.com/category/news-trends/podcasts

The Jewelry Podcast: shows.acast.com/the-jewelry-podcast

Thrive By Design: flourishthriveacademy.com/podcast/

Connect with Nicole

For more information about Nicole and her jewelry, events, in-person workshops, and video tutorials (from which the videos in this book are excerpted), visit her website: nicoleringgold.com

To see more of Nicole's work, visit her Instagram account: @ringgoldnicole

Acknowledgments

I could not have embarked on this project without my creative and diligent daughter Cymone Lenio. Mona, how can I adequately express my gratitude for your countless hours photographing my process and editing for this publication? Your patience is inspiring. I love you to the moon and around every single star to infinity.

To my beloved Derek for believing in me, trusting, and knowing that I could. It was your nudge that helped catapult me into this wild world of silversmithing. How could we have imagined where it would lead? Thank you for being my biggest fan and advocate. I love you more.

Cymone (left) and Nicole.

About the Author

Nicole Ringgold is a silversmith living in Winthrop, Washington, located in the North Cascade mountains. Her art is inspired by her natural surroundings: plants she encounters while hiking through the mountains, the shapes of rocks she plucks from a river, a sound, glimpse, or smell. Her botanical jewelry is hand fabricated, not cast, dipped, or electroformed. She starts with silver sheets and wire, sawing, soldering, filing, texturing, forming, oxidizing, and polishing every piece. Her intention is to recreate natural forms in silver with as much detail as possible, with the goal of making the metal appear alive. She teaches silversmithing workshops in her home studio and around the world. For more about Nicole's work, workshops, and tutorials, visit nicoleringgold.com and @ringgoldnicole on Instagram.

About the Photographer

Cymone L. Van Marter is currently a junior in the Honors College at the University of Arizona. She is double majoring in Film and Television and East Asian Studies, with minors in both Korean and Spanish. She is passionate about photography, travel, and language, and hopes to incorporate all three into a career upon completion of her degree. When at home in the Pacific Northwest, she fills her soul by exploring the trails throughout the North Cascade mountains with her parents and chocolate lab.

Index